VOLUME TWO

Secrets

of the

Most Holy Place

Secrets
of the
Most Holy Place

Discovering
the Wonders of the
Christ Within

DON NORI

Destiny Image® Publishers, Inc.

P.O. Box 310
Shippensburg, PA 17257-0310

"We Publish the Prophets."

ISBN 0-7684-2175-6

For Worldwide Distribution
Printed in the U.S.A.

This book and all other Destiny Image, Revival Press, MercyPlace, Fresh Bread, Destiny Image Fiction, and Treasure House books are available at Christian bookstores and distributors worldwide.

1 2 3 4 5 6 7 8 9 10 / 09 08 07 06 05 04

For a U.S. bookstore nearest you, call
1-800-722-6774.

For more information on foreign distributors, call
717-532-3040.

Or reach us on the Internet:
www.destinyimage.com

Table of Contents

In the Holy Place, God breaks Himself down into components man understands. In the Most Holy Place, man is broken down into components that God can use.

Mercy and truth are met together; righteousness and peace have kissed each other.

Psalm 85:10

*Let me be
who I am.
Release me to
discover His
wonders.*

CHAPTER 1

Just T'row the Ball!

I knew he had something exciting to tell me. I could see it in his huge brown eyes as I pulled into the driveway that beautiful spring evening after work. As usual, the other boys raced to the car with the tales of adventure and intrigue that filled their day, all talking and laughing at the same time. Soon, having stolen sufficient hugs and kisses for the time being, they ran off to discover who-knows-what in the wooded fields behind our home.

Then there was Joel. After patiently waiting for his brothers, he walked up to me with anticipation and excitement in his eyes. He was only seven, but his eyes always told a dozen stories and revealed a hundred secrets. He walked up to me and threw his arms around me.

"Dad, guess what?"

"Hi, Joel, what do you want me to guess?"

"Guess what I want to do?"

"Hmmm, guess what you want to do..."

"I want to play baseball! I was talking to my friend, and he's playing and he wants me to play too."

"Baseball! That's great son! That's awesome."

"Dad." Joel's face suddenly looked worried. "I don't know how to play baseball."

I couldn't help laughing. "That's OK, son. I will teach you. Tomorrow is Saturday. We'll start tomorrow."

Joel was so excited. We rummaged through the garage until we found all the necessary equipment for a good series of lessons. Back outside, Joel grabbed the bat and held it over his shoulder. "I want to hit the ball," he said with devilish determination.

I laughed.

He stood in front of me swinging the bat so hard it nearly knocked him over. I started to review all the basics of the game. There was so much to talk about, so much he needed to know.

I talked on as I held the ball in my hand. Joel practiced the dozens of poses he had seen the pros do. He bent his knees and wiggled his little behind. He leaned over and stood up tall. He spit in his hands and rubbed them in the dirt, then wiped them on his legs. He was already playing baseball.

"Why do guys spit in their hands?" he interrupted me.

"It helps them grip the bat," I responded, watching him peel the mud from between his fingers. "But they don't usually spit that much in their hands."

"Kinda gross," he mumbled as he knelt down and tried to wipe his hands clean on the grass.

"Pay attention now, son."

"Sure, Dad," he said as he rubbed the bat under his arm like the big guys do.

I didn't realize he had no idea what I was saying. He was riveted with the anticipation of swinging that stick and hearing the crack of the bat as the ball soared over the house and beyond.

Nonetheless, there was so much he needed to know. I just talked on, quite proud of everything I knew about the game and completely absorbed in my exhaustive presentation.

The sound of a small boy whimpering interrupted my discourse. I was aghast as I saw Joel standing in front of me crying. Only moments before he was having so much fun with the prospect of swinging the bat. Now he was leaning on it as he cried.

"What's the problem, Joel? I thought you were excited about learning to play baseball. I thought you wanted me to teach you to—"

"Just t'row the ball, Dad! T'row the ball!"

I was shocked and embarrassed. I suddenly realized that the learning would come with the playing. In fact, learning seemed secondary to his desire to play. But playing would increase his desire to learn.

Well, I dropped the ball and gathered him in my arms. As always during times of childhood trauma, he buried his face in my neck. I couldn't help but laugh at myself.

"Was Daddy talking too much?"

He never said a word, but I could feel his head nodding.

"I am so sorry, son. Come on, now, pick up that bat and let's see how far you can hit this ball."

In an instant, he jumped down from my arms, grabbed the bat, put it over his shoulder, and looked at me as that familiar devilish grin crossed his face. He was about to hit that ball to kingdom come or fall down trying, but he was going to be playing baseball.

We Are All Waiting to Play Ball

Joel is not the only one who is waiting to play ball. I can remember sitting in more church meetings than I can count, just waiting for the preacher to "t'row the ball." In fact, like my son, I have been exasperated to tears as apparently crucial instruction was given in drone-like perfection week after week, month after month, and year—well, you get the picture.

The Church has been waiting for years for someone to just shut up and "t'row the ball." We have believed in authority and patiently waited for men and women of God to release us into all God has dreamed for us. We have waited to be released by the power of the prophetic word that sets the heart ablaze with the possibility of doing the will of God and fulfilling our destiny at long last.

Nonetheless, believers are still waiting for someone to empower them. We are waiting for someone to remind us that God loves us and not only has a dream for us as individuals, but fully intends to see those dreams come to pass while we are able to do something about them. But, alas, the ball cannot be thrown by the worn and tired prayers of a clueless religious system, or the eloquent sermons that are presented with breathless precision. The ball cannot be thrown by men who build their own kingdoms and are buried in their own insecurities. The ball will never be thrown by hirelings who are primarily concerned with their own positions and their own futures.

Who Wants to Play Ball?

The ball can only be thrown by people who want you to play the game. It can only be thrown by those who are more interested in the Church than their own egos. The leaders who want you to participate have no agenda and no fear of being out played. They are not afraid of throwing the ball to a better player. They only rejoice that Christ will be more magnificently displayed. These folks have only one goal. They are desperate for the reality and love of Christ Jesus Himself, Who is the Bread of Life to the nations and the Living Water that quenches the thirsty soul.

We Will "T'row the Ball"

We can say this so confidently because Jesus already threw the ball when He gave Himself for us and rose so victoriously from the dead. You are the priests of the Presence. You are the royal priesthood, the holy nation. You are already the ministers of His glory whether or not you are ever recognized or ordained by anyone. He has seen you, recognized you and called you to Himself. You may never stand in a pulpit or teach a Sunday school class, but you minister His Presence because He lives in you. The dream God has dreamed for mankind can only be fulfilled when we all step forward and become everything that He has placed in our hearts to be as individuals.

Some of you will be ready for this; others will be caught looking in another direction. But we will "t'row the ball."

Many of us are waiting for the opportunity, the possibility of intimate fellowship, friendship, and service to our Lord that will last for the rest of our lives. You are the ones who understand that you are priests of the Presence, the Body of Christ, the Melchezidek of God. You are God's intended instrument of mercy, love, and salvation. You are the lamp in whom dwells the Light of the World.

The Beginning of Dreams

For what God has done for us is not the sum of our dreams. It is the beginning of them. It is not the final destination; it is where we discover the dream He has for us and then agree with that dream.

This Most Holy Place is certainly where we rest in Him, but it is far from a resting place.

For from this position of attentive eagerness, He speaks what we have longed to hear. It is in this place that we are quick to say yes to what He wants. He launches us with His faith, His power, and His confidence. We soon find our lives full of meaning and purpose. But it is not the Most Holy Place that brings ultimate fulfillment. Ultimate fulfillment is found by doing the will of God once we have experienced this place of profound peace. This makes life worth living, no matter what it might be that He has dreamed for you.

No, I will not lie and tell you that not playing will cost your salvation, for then I would be no different from the religious taskmasters who force their desires on us through fear and intimidation. No, resisting Him will not cost your salvation, but it may cost your sense of fulfillment and joy as you see His Kingdom established around you instead of through you.

This is not a call to church as we have known it. It is a call to His Presence and to the Church that He is building, whatever on this planet that may be.

This will be a different challenge. It is not a challenge simply to agree with the words that are written. It is a challenge to allow that fire of heart that these words will undoubtedly ignite, to cause you to move beyond hearing and even beyond believing. These words should move you into doing, thus finding yourself in the very center of His work on this planet.

But I have every confidence in you. I remember you from the first *Secrets* book.

Yes, you are just like me. The fact is, I wrote this book for you.

I know your heart.

It still gives you away.

Chapter 1 Scripture References

Matthew 28:18-20 PEB   Matthew 6:10 PEB
John 3:16 NAS   John 6:56 PEB
I Corinthians 1:28 NIV   Matthew 5:14-16 PEB

*For what God has done for us is
not the sum of our dreams. It is the
beginning of them.*

There is
Someone
within who
believes in me
and will not
let me
give up.

CHAPTER 2

The Secret of Being Possessed

I have a confession to make.

I am possessed by a foreign entity.

There is something living in me that is not of this world, and I dare say is not of any world in this dimension.

It is not every day that one discovers a being from beyond the galaxy living inside of him. If this had not happened to me, I would have dismissed it as science fiction drivel, the sort of thing that makes a great story but has no basis in fact.

But this is fact.

An intelligent life form is living and moving inside of me, trying to control me, trying to convince me to do its work on this planet. It is a compelling force, far more powerful than can be possibly imagined.

If the truth really be told, my God, I have no idea what would happen to me if I would let this entity take full control of me. What would happen if I just gave in to it? What would happen if I no longer resisted its enticing, sometimes mesmerizing attempts to get me to lay down my guard long enough to have its way?

I wonder what would happen to me?

I wonder what would happen to everyone around me?

To those I work with?

To my family?

To the world?

Really, this thing inside me is like nothing you have ever imagined. It is, without exaggeration, not of this universe, not even of this dimension. But nonetheless I hear its voice. It haunts me day and night.

When I go to bed, the voice is there to trouble me as I drift off to sleep. Throughout the night, this voice often agitates my sleep, whispering, "I want you. I want you. I'm going to consume you. I'm not going to stop."

When I awaken in the morning, its haunting words continue relentlessly as they did throughout the night hours: "You don't know what it took for Me to get inside of you. You don't know what I had to do. You don't know what I had to sacrifice to get where I am, and I'm not going to give up. You have no hope to get rid of Me. You can try, but I'm not going anywhere."

Over the years, I have felt this being's movements within and heard its archaic attempts to communicate with me.

This is neither fiction or fantasy. It is the true reality of my life. I have been invaded by an alien life form that has taken up what appears to be permanent residence within my body.

I am possessed.

I am sorry if some you are frightened by this.

I wish it were not so.

Sometimes I wish I could simply ignore it and move on.

But I cannot.

Not a Random Act

This intelligent life form possesses me. It has its own mind. It has its own desires. It has its own plan. In fact, I have come to believe that this entity has possessed me, not as a random act for its own personal survival, but because I have somehow been especially selected by it. Strange as it may seem, I am convinced that it observed me from another dimension and personally chose to use me for who knows what reason. It saw me as I was formed in my mother's womb. It watched as my personality, my talents—everything that makes me, me—were intricately woven in the very fabric of my being. It was there and watched it happen.

It chose me. Can you imagine that? Now it wants to rule me, to control me. It picked me out before I was born, from another dimension, attached a dream to me, and said, "I'm going to get inside of that one."

With each passing day, this entity grows in its possession of me in every way. It seems to be requiring every part of me to accomplish its will.

I have, of course, no idea what it feels like to be pregnant, but I do know what it feels like to have something living and moving within, vying for my concentration amidst all the other things that clamor for my attention.

I can feel the Presence inside of me. It makes my heart churn with feelings I have never had and cannot explain. It makes me impatient with the average, with the normal expectations of life. I have become intolerant of single-dimension thought and perspectives that merely re-define what already is while ignoring what could be, what should be. I am beginning to see as it sees.

Bigger Than Me

This entity challenges every thought, every desire, every ambition. I do not know whether to fear it or release myself to it. I cannot decide whether to resist its persistent beckon or allow it total access to my heart and soul. In one way, its power and possibilities are beyond comprehension, certainly more than anything a normal person could ever hope to imagine, let alone experience. But in another way, its single-minded determination makes me fear the consequence of relinquishing control to its consuming resolve.

Everything inside of me says to trust this being without question or hesitation. Yet, everything inside of me also resists the possibility of giving control over to someone else, even if that Someone has the ability to fulfill my deepest hopes and dreams. Oh, the irony! Everything I have ever imagined is within my grasp, if only I will give over everything to the One who possesses my soul, trusting in Someone I cannot control.

Sometimes when I touch somebody, even accidentally, unless I'm careful He'll just leap out into the one I have touched. It is as though He has this desire, this one tracked mind to attach destiny to everyone He can possess. I am nothing special. He is not content to possess only me, but everyone who will drop his guard long enough to allow Him entrance.

It is as though He has a message.

It is as though His dimension holds the key to fullness of life in this dimension.

It is as though He wants to speak to the nations Himself.

It is as though He wants me to stretch out my hands, so He can touch the nations for Himself.

It is as though when I stretch out my hand and touch the nations, He is not only touching the nations but also with quiet and silent precision moving into the ones I touch.

It is as though He can only touch what I am willing to touch; He only embraces what I am willing to embrace.

It is as though the only smile He has is my smile, the only voice He has is my voice, and the only hug He has is my hug.

It is as though He wants to live His life through me.

It is as though He would express Himself fully through me, if only I will say 'yes' to Him more completely each day.

It is as though this entity from another dimension has a plan of love and healing for this planet that He wants to execute through me. He wants to transport the stuff of His realm into our dimension. He wants to deliver the power and life of His dimension into the hearts of those who will allow Him.

It is as though He knows more about our dimension than we do. It is certain that He needs nothing from us. Ours is by far the inferior dimension.

He draws all He needs from the dimension from which He comes. For the stuff He brings with Him has a power that seems almost magical. The rules of His realm defy the very laws of nature, the laws that most certainly control us, keeping us bound to this dimension and this order of things.

But there are other dimensions, other orders, other rules by which those of other dimensions are governed and by which some in this realm have had the courage to embrace and experience. For these, life has taken on a much different purpose, a much larger—dare I say superior?—reason to live.

We Can Touch Other Dimensions

For there are some who are content to dwell within the confines of this dimension. They are content with life on this level alone. But we are multi-dimensional beings who are constructed to communicate and pass freely from one dimension to another. The inner ache that so many feel from deep within is the call to another dimension. It is an invitation to experience life and fellowship in this higher place.

It is as though this entity is from the dimension of eternity. It is as though He is the Son of God, brooding over the earth once again, this time looking for ordinary people like you and me through whom He can live, move, and complete the plan of His Father. He comes on behalf of a broken and hurting people who search desperately for life, meaning, and fulfillment.

It is as though He would show us things beyond our wildest imaginations, if only we would give in to Him.

It is as though He is waiting for us to say yes.

Another Confession

Now I have another confession to make. This may also startle the unprepared, the religious, the complacent among us. But I will tell you anyway.

It's not so bad, this being possessed.

In fact, now that I know who possesses me and I am discovering why, it is beginning to be most exciting. I want to listen more carefully and keep myself prepared and unencumbered so I can be swift to respond to His voice. The things of this realm that were once so important are not so valuable to me. I simply do not need them.

Desperate to be Available to Him

I never quite know what will happen from day to day. Sometimes I am not sure what will happen from minute to minute. But I am always sure it will be incredible for me and life-changing for those to whom I am sent. So it is critical for me to be unfettered from the distractions of this dimension that prevent me from being ready to respond to His voice.

He does not see limitations and He does not confine Himself to the religious boundaries of mere mortals.

I realize that this other-dimensional entity, this Christ of God who possesses me, will send me to the most unusual places for the most unpredictable reasons in order to complete His will in the earth. I am in His control. The only boundaries that exist are the ones I assign to myself. He does not see limitations nor confine Himself to the religious boundaries of mere mortals. In fact, He has no boundaries like those imposed by a reluctant and frightened humanity. His landscapes are boundless and eternal. His dreams transcend time and offer only the most awesome of possibilities.

We constantly look for ways to restrict His movement, all in accordance with His Word, of course. He, on the other hand, is forever unveiling the same Word in ways that open our hearts and minds to the potential that has never been imagined.

The Outrageous of God

We have never really stopped to consider the outrageous as it fleets through our spirit. We are afraid of the outrageous because it threatens our security, so we have trained our-selves to reject the outrageous before it has time to upset the established order of things. But the outrageous is born in the heart of God. He thinks outside of time and space. His plan is born in the dimension from which He comes. Man rejects the thoughts of God because man considers the work of God from the confines of his own dimension, limited by logic and his own five senses. These cannot touch the dimension of spirit nor understand the rules that govern there.

Humanity just does not get it.

When God speaks from His dimension, He fully intends to complete what He has started with the stuff of His dimen-sion. He does not need our "stuff," for anything we put toward the effort is grossly inadequate. He does not even need our faith. He has His own faith that He brings with Him when He possesses us.

He only needs our cooperation.

He only needs for us to say yes to Him.

We reject the outrageous because it cannot be justified by the rules that govern time and space. But when we reject the outrageous, we reject God.

He has much to say to us, much He wants to do through us. His plans are made with all the power and creativity of His dimension. He brings everything He needs into time and space in order to bring it to pass. But we reject it because we choose not to consider the stuff of another dimension. We are therefore hopelessly bound to time, space, dirt, and death.

When we reject the out-rageous, we reject God.

What kind of a life is that? We are beings of this dimension who are equipped to yield to the work of a greater realm. Yet we allow ourselves to be controlled by those whose minds are permanently bound to this finite realm of death and failure.

It is really most simple. Christ wants to change the world Himself. He wants to build His own Church and His own Kingdom.

He wants to tell His own story.

He wants to exalt His own Father and show the world how wonderful it is to be possessed.

We Yield, He Moves

He has possessed us to live His life through us. We do not need to play the games of religion that have no idea of the power and determination of the One who lives within us.

It is not hard when you understand that He wants to show Himself to us with far more passionate determination than we can imagine. He wants to show Himself to us that He may live His life through us. We do so many silly things to try to get His attention! But He does not need convinced. We already have His attention.

Getting His Attention

I do not have to sing, read, fast, pray, dance, cry, or fall over to get His attention. I do not have to beg, make deals, or use formulas to convince Him to listen to me. In the past, I thought He was a disinterested party helping me because He either had to, was forced to, or took pity on such a miserable life form such as me. That is the way I was taught.

But that is not the way it is at all!

He spied me out! He set the plan in motion to possess me even when I was not aware of it. He wants to get on with the business of using me for His plan. He wants me to hear and respond as quickly as I can. I only need to grow quiet enough to hear His voice. What I thought were His archaic attempts to talk to me were really His attempts to communicate with a life form far too busy with his own needs and desires to respond to Him Who lives within.

He Brings Everything He Needs

He needs nothing from me. In truth, everything He needs to change this dimension comes from His dimension. Nothing from this realm has the power or ability to effect permanent, generational change in time and space as we know it. So He brings everything with Him from the dimension that sent Him. He brings all His own faith, His own wisdom, His own love, His own compassion, His own power as well as everything else that will be necessary to establish His own Kingdom among mortal man. We are talking about an awesome task here. He wants to build in us and among us, in this dimension the same benevolent Kingdom that is the life and shining star of the dimension from which He comes.

All that He brings, He brings in Himself, who now possesses me and all others who will agree with Him. He is setting up shop inside mere humanity. He is building immortality within those who are mortal. Two dimensions are touching, interacting. We are being affected, no, transformed by a dimension of spirit that dwells beyond the reach of our five senses, into a jurisdiction that flesh and blood cannot enter and certainly has no authority in apart from this Christ of God. There, the law is simple. You enter, dwell, fellowship, and grow by the substance of spirit. Entrance by any other means is impossible.

True Possession

This is a near religious experience, but it has nothing to do with religion. A religious experience in this dimension can be faked. One can claim that he is possessed when really he is only pretending to be possessed. This is quite common among men in this dimension. Although why someone would pretend to have what he can have in reality is quite beyond my limited understanding. If one only pretends to be possessed, he must act as though he is, while having nothing from that dimension that really changes the heart or empowers him to his destiny. A bad situation just gets worse when a false confession leads to false demonstration of something one does not really have. It gets more and more complicated.

Hmmm. That, I guess, is a true religious experience.

I cannot imagine why anyone would want to fake being possessed. What? You are laughing as though I am crazy. But it happens every day. People who are not possessed pretend to be possessed while criticizing and judging those who truly are possessed. They try to make everyone think they are in league with this Christ of God, doing His bidding and hearing His voice, but all the while they fear those who are possessed by Him.

These spiritual hucksters secretly plan the spiritual, emotional, and physical demise of those who are allowing this entity to do His work through them. These are the same people who begin to see the vast and unlimited provision from this other dimension and attempt to use its assets for their own profits and for their own personal kingdoms, even when it means siphoning assets from those believers who are unaware of their deception.

We do not play the games of religious hucksters who have no idea of the power and determination of the One who lives within us.

Those not truly possessed exact burdens and duties that have nothing to do with true possession upon the innocent. These folks know the right words but cannot deliver the love, compassion, or power of the eternity. Rather, they only imitate the nature of Christ and place themselves in positions of authority they have neither earned nor understood.

True possession is something else altogether. True possession is the living and vibrant activity of Christ within a person's body, soul, and spirit. This life form is constantly transferring to the ones He possesses the incredible supply of everything that makes His plan feasible in the human heart.

In these folks, nothing has to be faked because the power is from this other dimension and the work of changing the heart is not theirs. The work that goes on within is genuine and obviously the work of the entity that possesses them.

When weakness is discovered, one simply turns inward to the life form that possesses him. He is the One who has the power to strengthen the weak place. So there is nothing to be ashamed of and nothing to run from. The Christ of God is at work within them to do the will of God and to transform them into all they are intended to be.

I know, I know. Some think that with everything inside that needs changed, this entity would most likely throw you right out the door. The problem is that He is already in you. He has already poured so much into you that to discard you would mean throwing out all the work He has already done. He cannot discard Himself. So even if you are faithless, He must remain faithful to Himself.

But I have discovered a wonderful thing. He has the power to alter anything in this dimension, including me. I cannot keep myself right. I cannot change myself. There is nothing in this dimension of time and space with the power to permanently change me.

Fear doesn't change me. Fear just discourages me.

Guilt doesn't work. Guilt only makes me feel hopeless. Totally hopeless.

Shame is a fraud. It merely causes me to turn away from the One I love.

Condemnation is a bitter lie. It tells me the One to Whom I have given everything has rejected me because I have failed.

These are the empty tools of lifeless religion. They are the finite accusations of those who do not know the infinite glory and wonder of true possession.

Hope for Today

But I do hear something within my heart that I am certain comes straight from Him. It is the song of hope. I hear Him saying to me again and again, "I will change you. Do not fear. I will change you. You might not yet be what you want to be, but I promise I will change you into what I want you to be. You focus on the world, and I will focus on you. You give yourself to listening to me and saying yes, and I will transform you from the inside out. For I AM working on you from where I live—inside of you."

Therefore, at this point in my life, without apology, without fear, without shame, I have come to realize and I am thrilled to tell everyone, "I am possessed by the living Christ of God. Not my will, but His will be done."

Chapter 2 Scripture References

Hebrews 1:3 NKJV

Romans 12:2 PEB

John 16:8 NKJV

I Peter 2:9 NKJV

Jeremiah 1:5 NKJV

Proverbs 3:5 NKJV

I John 1:2 PEB & NKJV

Romans 6:23 PEB

I Corinthians 13:8 PEB

Romans 8:5-8 PEB

Acts 9:15 NIV

Philippians 2:5-11

I am happy to announce to the world, without apology, without fear, without shame, "I am possessed by the living Christ of God."

He will change me, while I change the world.

CHAPTER 3

The Secret to Changing the World

Incredible possibilities open up once I understand that this Christ of God lives in me as completely as I live in my own home. He wants to inhabit me, prepare me, and use me just as completely as I do my house. He wants me to hear Him, understand Him, respond to Him, say "yes" to Him. He wants me to interact with Him moment by moment. For He actually has taken up residence in me with the purpose of changing the world through me.

I have realized that the best hope I have of making a significant and lasting contribution to the world is in allowing Him to have His way in me.

I must say 'yes' to him daily.

This Life is worth fighting for.

I will contend for it.

I will not allow His Life to be taken away or explained away by anyone, not even by myself.

Tomorrow holds a hope that few could ever imagine and that even fewer expect could be experienced. But it can be experienced. That is what salvation is all about.

Heaven is my destination; it is not my destiny. Many will reach their destination, but few will fulfill their destiny.

I am destined to be conformed to His precise image and likeness. He will be magnified through these old bones by the work of the cross and the dream He has dreamed for me, now, in this life.

Heaven is my destination; it is not my destiny.

But I look at the condition of the house He lives in and determine that I am not fit to be or to do what He wants.

However, there is a problem with my thinking.

A big problem.

He has already moved in.

He has already chosen me.

Of course, I do not understand how this could be. Everywhere I look inside I see trouble.

The walls of my heart have been papered with layers of fear and guilt.

My mind is a landfill of anger and unbelief.

My spirit is untouchable with pock holes of argument and distrust.

My spirit is caramelized with envy, greed, and the lust for power.

My memory is breaking down trying to hold onto grudges and hurts long since past into eternity.

I see what a serious investment it would take to make this old house livable for the divine Presence.

To be honest, I have secretly agreed with the counsel of all those who analyze me, determining if this old house is worth the makeover. Most of them decided I was just not worth the time, the effort, and the money it would take to do even marginal improvements within me. It was no surprise to me when so many just turned and walked away, shaking their heads with the overwhelming confidence that I was definitely not worth the investment.

But this One who possesses me, who purchased me, who moved in knowing exactly what He was getting into, I do not understand.

Having been rejected so often and by so many others, how could He be right about me? How could He want me?

Well, I guess He knows what He is getting Himself into. He evidently had a tour of this old house before He decided to buy it. He knew I was a "handyman's special." You know, a polite way of advertising that you'd better be ready for severe disappointment before you walk through this place. But He did not need a walk-through. He knew I was going to be a real fixer-upper. Nonetheless, He paid the asking price and moved right in, without any regrets, I might add.

Unlike others who saw me and rejected me immediately, He did not just see what I was. He did not consider what others had seen as they ravaged my heart, my emotions, my life. He saw what I could be under the right ownership. He saw what a showcase of His love and mercy I could be, given the right interior designer. He understood how I could be just right for the dream He dreamed for me. He saw how I could most completely assist Him in accomplishing His purpose for me on this planet.

"Your Job is to Change the World."

So now this changes everything for me. I am shocked, gratified, and humbled. But most of all, relieved. At least there is Someone who sees something in me worth remodeling and using.

"Son,"

I often hear Him say, "Let Me worry about changing you. You give yourself to changing the world."

What a deal. He will remodel the house while I get to entertain the guests He sends.

It is quite exhilarating to know I am working together with One who sees such potential in me. I want more than ever to quiet myself so I can hear Him. I will give myself to distinguishing my voice from His voice. I want to discern my will from His; my emotions, desires, and plans from His.

Quiet My Heart

I want to distinguish the noise of the world from the song of the Lord.

For the first time in my life, quietness and holiness make sense. I do not pursue holiness to get to heaven. I pursue it because it is a place of quiet and calm. For holiness is far from the clanging sounds that engulf the voice of the Lord and make His voice indistinguishable from all the clutter that life and religious conditioning bring into my soul.

If am to do what He wants, if I am to hear things I have never heard, I need to be in a quiet place. This is a place of spirit, where the distractions of flesh, religion, and the enemy cannot live. Without this place of spiritual quiet, I hear all my detractors, who will only keep me weary, guilty, defeated, and most certainly unfulfilled.

But I can recognize His voice.

The old voice reminds me of my failures while the voice of the Lord reminds me of who I am. The old voice heaps guilt and regret upon me while the voice of the Lord strips guilt from my heart, allowing the light of His forgiveness to flow deep inside where I want Him the most.

The voice of religion resists and denies the work of the Lord inside me and even resists the possibility of the Presence of such a being within.

The voice of intellect requires reason and logic to be the plumb line of my experience. Assuming, of course, that single-dimensional reason can ever begin to answer the mystery and wonder of an extra-universal being who has arrived on this planet for reasons we can only accept by faith and respond to with hope and anticipation.

Contending for this Life

I will contend for this. I will contend for the reality that is the living, risen Christ within. I will not contend for religious intellectualism that exalts and enthrones itself upon Dagon's lofty seat. Presiding over a failed system, these self-appointed judges of all that is religious continue to ordain themselves into the service of a system that resists the Presence. It denies the power of God in the life of the individual in whom the Presence has taken up permanent residence. For Dagon's lofty throne is a doomed kingdom. Dagon is dashed to the ground in a thousand pieces when the light of the Presence is raised above his arrogance.

All the money, supercilious intimidation, and fleshy superiority they can gather will never secure a system that is destined to fail. It is toppled in the night season of our lives, for it fails us when we need it most. It offers no hope, no power, and no answers in our most desperate hour of need.

Yes, I will contend for this Life, this power, this eternal love that is committed to my future, my success, and my reason to live.

"You go change the world," He says so confidently to me. "I will change you."

I am beginning to understand that this One who lives within me draws me to a place of clarity and peace. He draws me to a place where I can hear His voice as well as know He can hear mine. It is the place of "yes," in the dimension of all-God. It is the place where two dimensions touch, where eternity seems to sag into time and space, affecting everything within its reach. It is the place where He speaks and nature responds quickly, confidently, and totally.

"You go change the world," He says so confidently to me, "I will change you."

In this place, the silly things we have done in the past to entice Him to listen to us no longer make sense, for we see His single-minded intention for union with mere human beings. We try so hard to maintain the sense of His Presence, to feel His love, when He has already taken up residence within us. Permanently.

We do not have to prove ourselves. He already proved us through His Son. When we give ourselves to this realm of surrender, this realm of all-God, rest and peace sweep in. Instead of worrying, struggling, and performing the antics of religion's diabolical intentions, we begin to sense the Presence inside—living, growing, waiting.

Stay the Course

When the Apostle Peter denied Jesus, he ran to the familiar. He ran to his past. Jesus knew right where to find him. Peter was consumed with his failure. He was certain that he was now disqualified from doing the will of God and thus also disqualified from fulfilling the destiny God had for him.

But Peter was the only one who was surprised at his failure. Jesus had used him for three years knowing his weakness. Jesus' response was predictable. That is, it was predictable as we consider His mercy for others. Most of the time we are certain that His mercy does not extend to us.

"Peter," Jesus said to him, "get back into town and do the will of God."

"But, Lord, I failed You. I don't love You like I thought I did."

Sounds familiar, doesn't it?

"Peter, I know you. I know what is inside of you. You are forgiven. You are loved with a love that your failure cannot destroy. Now, get back into town and do the will of God."

"Jesus, I denied You. I committed a most despicable act. You must know I cannot do this."

Peter made the classic mistake of thinking that change depended on him. When he realized he could not change himself, he wanted to quit. And he did.

I can imagine Peter remembering the times he responded to situations in the strength of his own flesh. In the Presence of His Lord, of course!

He remembered wanting to build three tabernacles on the mountain where Jesus showed him Moses and Elijah. That memory was so painful. Then there was the time he rebuked the Lord and would not accept the possibility of crucifixion; he pulled his sword and shed blood in the Garden of Gethsemane. Only hours later, after showing such courage and determination, he failed again. He denied the Lord he loved so desperately. He ran. The memories crowded his heart as he wept before his Lord.

"Peter, you don't have the power to change yourself. The truth is, you cannot change yourself under any circumstances. It is not your job to change yourself. It is My job to change you."

Jesus looked ever so gently into Peter's eyes.

"But you have a job, Peter. A very important job. Your job is to change the world. So, let's make a deal."

I can just see Peter looking at Jesus with a bit of confusion.

"A deal?"

"A deal," Jesus said. "I will do My job, and you can do yours. I will change you, and you go change the world."

"You go change the world, and I will change you."

The secret is so simple.

We are called to change the world.

He came to change us.

39

Chapter 3 Scripture References

Psalms 140:13 NAS
Matthew 5:6 PEB
Matthew 11:28-30 PEB
Luke 24:32 PEB
Colossians 1:24 NKJV

Revelation 21:6 PEB
Romans 10:9-10 NKJV
Hebrews 11:1 PEB
Matthew 6:14 PEB

He did not consider what others had seen as they ravaged my heart, my emotions, my life. He saw what I could be under the right ownership.

*I am not
a mistake of
nature. I am
hungry for
God.*

CHAPTER 4

The Secret of Spiritual Hunger

The screen door slammed shut with a bang as the boys chased their newest pet out of the kitchen and into the back yard. I will never forget the excitement that little kitten created among our five boys as they ran and played and laughed and shouted. They watched with wonder as their newest pet licked its paws, drank milk from a small bowl, and wiped its little face. Together, they thoroughly enjoyed doing all the things that kittens and kids do in the course of a hot summer day.

But evening came far too soon. Mom called in the troops to wash up for dinner. The table was noisy with dozens of stories from the day's adventures with their newest companion.

I would never let them know it, me not being the animal lover their mother had instilled in their hearts to be, but that was the cutest fur ball I had ever seen. It curled itself up in your arms and purred ever so quietly, always looking for a place to bury its head. Its meow was quiet and sweet. The kitten would reach up to your face with its tiny paw as though reassuring itself that it was safe enough to go to sleep. No wonder there was a nightly argument as to whose bed it would get to spend the night in. But that argument turned to sadness one evening when the kitten just seemed to vanish. In the excitement of the day, no one thought to bring the kitten into the house. So the entire family went

43

kitty hunting in the darkness of the summer evening, lit only by the moon, tiny flashlights, and fireflies.

But the kitten was nowhere to be found. The search was called off with the promise of beginning the hunt again at the crack of dawn. Proper prayers of protection, safety, and warmth were offered by kids whose eyes still swelled with tears. After which they all drifted off to sleep.

Monday is always the worst day of the week. It means their special playmate, Dad, has to get up early and be off to work, far too early for hugs and kisses from the kids.

But as he walked out of the house, he was startled by the faint but certain sound of a kitten calling out for help. We still really don't know how it ended up under a bucket, but the kitten was soon rescued from its prison, into which it was incarcerated by who-knows-who sometime the day before. Dad gathered it in his arms and held it close. Mom went to get a bowl of milk.

"You are just about the sweetest little animal I have ever seen," Dad whispered while Mom was in the kitchen. After all, even in this situation, a man must protect his honor.

"I could get to like you," he said as Mom appeared in the doorway with the milk. Before Dad could finish whispering his sweet nothings to the kitten, it leaped onto Mom with a noise that I never knew a kitten could make. With claws extended, fangs visible, and hissing all the way, it attached itself to Mom with its claws, spilling the milk on the porch. After a second equally horrifying hiss, it pushed itself away from Mom, somersaulted onto the ground, and began voraciously licking up the milk.

We were stunned. Mom had several deep scratches on her arm and abdomen. Dad just shook his head. "I always said you could never trust a kitten."

What happened?

A gentle, cute little kitten had turned into an apparently mean, violent animal. It instinctively knew that to live, it had to find food. And it did. Nothing was going to stand in the way of its survival, no matter what it took, no matter how it appeared. It was their nature. It is ours as well.

44

Spiritually hungry people are no different. Soft and prayerful, sensitive and giving, they love, serve and honor. They are faithful and compassionate.

But they have spent far too many nights under a bucket.

They are starving too. Their response is also apparently strange. But hunger changes the nature of man and beast alike. Food becomes top priority to anyone who is starving.

They are most often misunderstood.

It has become the normal response to this genuine hunger toward God that these folks have to condemn them as rebellious, angry troublemakers. It has become too easy to see them as malcontents in the church and simply invite them to leave.

But these folks are not rebellious any more than that cute little kitten had malice in its heart the day it scratched and ran for food. Neither are these folks unruly. They are simply in need of their Lord's Presence and divine fellowship.

To be sure, there is ample space for concern when it comes to those in the Body of Christ who just cannot settle down. They easily find fault and are quick to accuse and walk away from fellowship.

We are not talking about that kind of person.

We are talking about gentle, loving folk who give, love, and would serve the local church with all their heart. They love God's people and will do anything the Lord asks them to do. They are usually the most willing of servants, the best givers, and the most faithful to the meetings. They love the safety and protection of the local church. They honor the pastor and the appointed leaders. All would be quite peaceful if not for one thing—hunger for God. For as we have seen with the kitten, hunger will change the character of anyone. Hunger will force a search for food that is often beyond the comfort zone of leaders who fear for themselves, their reputations, and their futures.

These folks hunger for true spiritual substance. They need Him, not a story about Him. They need true worship, not merely songs. They need His Manifest Presence, not an intellectual discussion about His Presence. They need to experience Him and Him alone. They need to be challenged and drawn to Him, encouraged and released into His service.

To be sure, those who are true to themselves will understand that something much deeper than rebellion is going on among these people. They understand that to accuse these folks of defiance or insubordination is as tragic as it is incorrect.

Hungry people need to be fed or they will go search for what they need for themselves. It is true that shipwreck is often their end as they wander through the maze of religion and legalistic control. Often finding their Lord apart from the religious system, they are condemned as heretics and left as outcasts among wolves who prey on their desperation and devour their strength and love. Their blood stains the souls of all those who judge them unfairly.

True Revolutionaries

There are those who labor among us that some do not understand. They strive according to a power many have not experienced. They respond to a Voice others have not heard. A voice that mightily works within them. These are rejected by world systems, pious religions, and fearful men. They are ones concerning of whom the world is not worthy, being possessed by a love that consumes and overwhelms them just as labor overwhelms a woman with child.

But some will recognize the fire in their eyes, the glory in their smiles, the hope in their conversation, the love in their service.

God sends them to the most unlikely places, among the most common of people. They carry the most precious of possessions to be given to the most unworthy of peoples. But they themselves are not recognizable by their wit or charisma. They offer no special talents, no wealth, and no particular favor, as the world judges.

But some will recognize the fire in their eyes, the glory in their smiles, the hope in their conversation, the love in their service. Some will hear their song even when they are not singing and see light in their lives even in the darkest of times.

Some see the Christ of God in them, controlling them and living His supernatural life through them. They will recognize that their impatience and near-rebellion is the impatience of the Lord, who came to move us beyond religion and human control into the glorious fulfillment of the sons of God.

David was looking at these folks when he said, "As for the saints who are in the earth, they are the majestic ones, in whom is all my delight."

Chapter 4 Scripture References

Matthew 5:6 PEB
Matthew 6:8 PEB
Ephesians 4:14 NKJV
Luke 6:25 PEB
John 8:32 PEB
Hebrews 10:22 NKJV

I Peter 2:2 NAS
Galatians 5:22 PEB
Romans 12:1 PEB
Romans 8:9 NKJV
Psalms 16:3 NKJV

But some will recognize the fire in their eyes, the glory in their smiles, the hope in their conversation, the love in their service.

*He holds
my weakness
in the palm
of His
hand.*

CHAPTER 5

The Secret of Iniquity and the Ten-Penny Nail

The same thing happened every school day morning. My twin brother, Ron, and I would grab our coats out of the closet off the old metal hangers and run down the driveway to catch our ride to school. The force of the coats being pulled off the hangers would send them flying in every direction as we slammed the closet door. We always had a good laugh listening to those old hangers banging around the closet as we ran out of the house.

Now, our family was never poor, but that was only because our parents were always so careful with everything we had. Our stuff always lasted much longer than it should have. In fact, if yard sales had been popular in those days, I am sure we never would have had one at our house. The things we had were used till they fell apart and glued together several times. They would have been totally useless to anyone else. So when Ron and I came home one night and found our two old metal coat hangers, bent like boomerangs and sitting on the kitchen table, we knew there was going to be a talk.

We couldn't help but laugh when we saw those hangers sitting there. They had finally had enough of our pulling at them, bending them, and sending them knocking around the closet every day. They were near the breaking point, pitiful looking if I would be honest.

Every time we pulled those coats off the hangers, it would put stress at the same spot. Over time, that one spot was just too weak to do its job. The inevitable happened. The hangers would bend right there when we pulled the coats off and bend again when we put the coats back on. It didn't matter that we were careful to straighten the hangers before we put the coats on them. Even the weight of the coats was enough to bend them. For a long time, though, we were able to make the hangers straight again so that it looked like nothing had ever been wrong. But then the metal began to turn white, a sign of the stress it was under each time we pulled a coat off. Even though we could get the hangers to straighten out, we would never get the color or the strength back into those old hangers.

Now, I don't know how much hangers cost in those days, but it didn't much matter—we were going to hear about it.

As was our custom when things looked bleak for us, we sat mischievously quiet, pretty close to angel-like as we heard Dad's old panel truck coming into the driveway.

I had no idea that he was about to teach me something that would turn out to be one of the most important lessons I would ever learn.

Dad walked up the stairs into the kitchen, where he knew we would be waiting.

"Hi, Dad, we had a great day at school today! Have any chores for us?"

"Right." We knew he was holding back a smile. He was that kind of dad.

"Boys, we are going to talk about these old hangers. You have to be careful how you treat them."

"Here goes," I always thought to myself.

One time, I kicked my brother under the table to get him to laugh, but he completely ignored me. So I kicked him again and again. I wanted him to be the first one to crack a smile. He was.

"Son." My dad turned to me. "Is there something wrong with your foot?"

"No, Dad."

"Then you better hold it still before you put a hole in my leg."

I froze, but he went on without another word to me.

"Boys, you just can't keep bending the hanger in the same spot like this. You are going to break it for sure. The metal just cannot handle that kind of treatment. Take care of it, be gentle, and it will stay strong forever."

"But, Dad, it's just a hanger." We tried not to laugh.

"It's not just a hanger. It has value and it can be fixed. If something can be fixed, boys, it's worth saving. Let me show you."

We followed Dad down to his workshop. He pulled two ten-penny nails out of an old coffee can and fired up his welder.

We watched as he carefully straightened out the hangers and then spot-welded the nails across the weakened part of both hangers. The weak area became the strongest part of the hanger. It was amazing, to be sure. I used that same hanger for years. It never bent there again. In fact, it was clearly the strongest part of the hanger.

I don't know what my dad understood about iniquity, but I got the message years later as I lamented before the Lord over my own struggle.

"That old hanger won't ever be strong there again," he said to us. "But that ten-penny nail will be its strength. It'll surely break somewhere else before it breaks where I just fixed it. The weakest part is now the strongest part."

I don't know what my dad understood about iniquity, but I got the message years later as I lamented before the Lord over my own struggle.

Iniquity Enters

The more I sin in a particular fashion, the weaker I get at that spot in my life. Temptation in that area then results in sin far more often as my ability to resist diminishes. I am like that old hanger that just keeps getting bent in the same way, time after time. I can be strong in so many other ways. But in the thing I give in to the most, my weakness grows. Temptation and sin are turned into iniquity there, a weakness toward a sin I cannot resist and certainly cannot overcome.

I need a ten-penny nail over that weak spot. I cannot protect myself there anymore. I have given in too many times. I need the power of the cross, my eternal ten-penny nail, welded over my weakness so I can be strong again. With this power of Christ Himself, I can now resist the very thing that enslaved me.

In the Holy Place, we just rebuke the devil and make as many excuses as are necessary to satisfy the conscience. But my weakness is forever weak, forever a place where I am certain to fall, forever a place where I come short of His glory.

My Ten-Penny Nail

But in the Most Holy Place, where the Mercy Seat calls to us and His power is made perfect in weakness, the work of Christ goes beyond our weak and fleshy attempts to make restitution and cover our own sins. For it is here that our confession, complete and without reservation, releases the power of God to become our ten-penny nail. Truly, where I was weak, I am now strong. Though I may occasionally fall, His mercy is ever present to wash me with His blood and gather me to Himself. Here, in His manifest Presence, I have no fear and therefore no need to make an excuse. His love overwhelms me and I am confident that I can confess my sin freely and without blame toward another. It is I who am responsible for my sin.

But here there is no condemnation and no fear. He will not condemn what He has redeemed. He will not scatter what He has gathered. I have passed from death to life. My weakness becomes my strength. My failure becomes a testimony of my hope, for He will never leave me.

Rather, His power gathers where I fail. He holds my weakness in the palm of His hand, strengthening me in my hope of deliverance.

Now, sin is no longer master over me. I am no one's slave, no one's puppet. My life is now and forever hidden in the Christ of God, whose power and deliverance was purchased for me completely on the cross. He is my hope and my strength. He is my ten-penny nail.

Chapter 5: Scripture Reverences

I Corinthians 15:31 NKJV

Hebrews 6:19 NKJV

Romans 12:2 NKJV

I Peter 2:9 PEB

I Peter 2:4 NKJV

I Corinthians 6:20 PEB

II Corinthians 5:14 NKJV

Revelation 2:7 PEB

Philippians 4:7 PEB

Revelation 7:17 NKJV

James 4:8 NKJV

John 13:38 PEB

John 14:6 NKJV

He holds my weakness in the palm of His hand, strengthening me in my hope of deliverance.

My heart
is the
greenhouse
in which
glory is
nutured.
It grows
within
me.

The Secret of His Glory

How long have we believed that glory is something mysterious and elusive? How long have we looked with great longing into the lives of those who have experienced His glory? We have tried, unsuccessfully, to content ourselves with seeing Him from afar, living in the hope that His glory would somehow become tangible to us as we go through life. We continuously try to earn enough favor that He might show Himself to us as He did to Moses or the three disciples on the Mount of Transfiguration. If only we could experience what the disciples experienced, we would be content in our walk with God. But we are quite certain we will never really measure up to the requirements.

Glory is not an award for the pious. It is grown in the heart of the broken.

Consequently, we have become comfortable with stories about His glory. At least the stories we hear prove to us that some have become worthy enough to experience the things that only angels and the truly spiritual do.

Where Glory Grows

But glory is not an award for the pious. It is grown in the heart of the broken.

Yes, the human heart is the greenhouse in which glory is nurtured. This supernatural "stuff" of the Spirit grows within us. It grows as mere mortal men and women die every day to the hidden desires that the fleshy part of us loves so secretly. When we die to the things we have been conditioned to think make us great, our hearts are melted into the dream God has dreamed for us. Glory, the spiritual substance of obedience, grows and oozes from us. It constantly woos everyone we come into contact with, to the Presence and love of God.

Glory is that wonderful substance of Spirit that is planted within us and grows as we yield to Him, saying, "yes" to Him every day.

Glory is the supernatural evidence that, quite literally, God is living inside the human body. It is not a prize for the so-called elite among us. In fact, glory eludes the one with the smell of earthy reputation and human effort. Rather, glory is the testimony of Jesus that shines from those who yield to Him.

As I mentioned in an earlier book, glory is convincing splendor. It is everything within a man that convinces the world that Jesus is Lord. We try to make this so complicated. But glory is not complicated. It is not reserved for the special believer or the leaders who preach His Word.

Glory is a supernatural event that happens most often without us being aware of its activity.

The glory of God flourishes among the humble of heart. It is not elusive or unattainable. Paul tried to tell us this so clearly when he warned us to be sure that no one falls short of His glory.

His glory is for the here and now. It is the normal outworking of His life among average people like you and me. The glory of God within us lifts the average to the remarkable and the weak to the strong. It shines with a gentle assurance that draws the nations to His light.

True Witnesses

Far from what we have been taught, witnessing is what we are rather than what we say. But some do not trust the glory within, so the only alternative is to talk. Yet, there is nothing more powerful than His Presence.

We are filled, possessed, consumed and ultimately shine with His Presence. He is genuinely living within us. He knows what to do with everyone we come into contact with. Our responsibility is to yield to Him who possesses us. Nothing more.

A woman recently asked me about her desire to minister in her job as a greeter at a major discount store in her city. She shined with the glory of God, and her eyes sparkled with God's love. But she was concerned that thousands of people walked by her each week, and most of them looked as though they needed the Lord in one way or another. She wanted permission from someone, anyone, to pass out a tract or to talk to as many folks as possible about the Lord.

But she already shined with the glory of the Lord.

"You are more than you could ever say," I began. "And you are light years ahead of anything you could hand to them.

"His Presence oozes from you with such vitality and life. There is healing in your smile and hope in your eyes."

Of course, the vitality, healing, and hope come from our Lord Jesus, who possesses this lady and flows from her so freely.

"You should trust the Holy Spirit that is within you and flows out of you," I said. "For the Lord is touching and healing and doing whatever He needs to do because you have brought Him to a place where He can do His own work among humanity. Who knows that the Lord has not placed you there just so He could touch the masses who pass by you each day. What a wonderful opportunity you have been given by taking a job where He can reach so many different people every day."

The woman wept at my response. In all her many years, she had never been told that God wants to live His life through her. She needed only to rest and allow His glory to shine through her.

Who Is the Glory For?

Paul tells us "Christ in you is the hope of glory". But whose glory? Is it for us or someone else?

Glory is not for us.

Glory is for those with whom we meet every day.

Christ in me is the hope of glory. Christ in me is the hope of those around me. Christ in me is the hope of a dying world, the healing of a broken home, the restoration of a shattered marriage.

Christ in me is the hope of the poor, the hope of the lonely, and the hope of those who are in despair.

Christ in me is the hope of those who wander into a discount store and just happen to come face-to-face with the Light of the World.

Christ in me, Christ possessing me, Christ living His life through me, changing the world through me, without limitations—without the boundaries of religion, tradition, and fear—is the hope of the world and the foundation of everything I have hoped for, prayed for, and desired in my life. Christ in me releases every dream and every possibility I can and cannot imagine.

Christ in me, without the controls of carnal men who are afraid of change and the power of God, will win the nations and bring them running to the place of His manifest Presence.

His glory is not about witnessing.

It is not about an evangelistic outreach.

His glory is about His manifest Presence convincing the world that He is truly Savior, Lord, and coming King. He does this from His own base camp that is called your heart.

Glory is His own activity. The work of man produces legalism and control, sweat and guilt. Glory produces life, peace, and joy unspeakable. The fruit of the Spirit is the by-product of His glory.

Glory is grown in a heart of brokenness.

Glory shines through you and me and convinces the world that Jesus is Lord.

The glory of the Lord will cover the earth as the water covers the sea. This will happen when you and I are blown by the Spirit of God to every corner of this planet, where His glory will be seen and experienced by every living creature.

"Arise, shine; for thy light is come, and the glory of the LORD is risen upon thee. For, behold, the darkness shall cover the earth, and gross darkness the people: but the LORD shall arise upon thee, and his glory shall be seen upon thee. And the Gentiles shall come to thy light, and kings to the brightness of thy rising."

Chapter 6 Scripture Reverences

I Corinthians 12:31 NKJV
Matthew 6:10 PEB
II Thessalonians 2:3 PEB
Galatians 15:22 PEB
Proverbs 3:5 NKJV

Psalms 37:3 NKJV
Luke 1:50 PEB
I John 4:13 NKJV
Matthew 6:14 PEB

Glory is the supernatural evidence that, quite literally, God is living inside the human body, mine.

My Father
will send
the rain.
It will
unite with
the River
within
me.

The Secret of the Rain

The sun was afire that summer afternoon as the farmer walked with his youngest boy through the fields of corn they had planted just before the spring rains came. They had thought this was going to be the best year in a long while. The rains had been heavy for almost three weeks. When the corn sprouted, it looked as though it had leaped from the ground as it reached through the crisp morning air to the brilliance of the sun.

But that was all the rain that came. Sure was beautiful though. As far as the eye could see, the sky was deep blue. There were a few days when high wispy clouds teased the father and son as they looked to the sky for more rain. But the rain just did not come. Now they walked through the rows of stunted cornstalks with the dust of the hardened earth swirling around their feet as they went.

The farmer's son chewed on the end of a weed, as kids do when they go through a field on a summer's afternoon.

The boy broke the silence when the old farmer knelt beside a cornstalk. "Neighbors are calling a prayer meeting," he said.

"The harvest rain will be too little and too late for this crop." The farmer spoke as though he did not hear his son. "We need water right now and we need the harvest rain too. That would save this corn, maybe even make it a good year." The old man squeezed an ear of corn as he spoke. "If it gets much bigger without the kernel, we are finished for this year."

"Dad, did you hear me? The neighbors are calling a prayer meeting tonight to ask the Lord for rain. Do you want to go? 'Cause if you do, Mom and I will go too."

The farmer turned to his youngest son, born a little late as kids go. All the others were near gone, grown up and starting their own lives. The ones left might as well be gone, as busy as they were with other things. Too busy for their own good.

"Yes," the farmer said, smiling, "we will go to the prayer meeting tonight."

"It's gonna be in the Cooper's barn after supper."

The farmer stood up and started back to the house. "We need help from the Lord, all right," he said almost to himself as they walked.

"Wouldn't it be cool if we could save the spring rain for the harvest? You know, just in case the harvest rain wasn't enough." His son was excited as they walked. He believed in the Lord and knew He would not let them down.

The farmer stopped dead in his tracks. "What'd you say, boy?"

"I was just joking, Dad," the boy said with a big smile. "I said I wished there was a way to save the spring rain for the harvest."

"Boy, I think I hear the Lord talking to me through your innocent little mouth." The farmer turned toward the barn to get a pick and shovel. He ran to the edge of the field where the creek bed was dry as dirt. "The spring rain is here," he thought to himself. "Leastwise, it's where it was the last time I saw it."

"But, Dad, what about the prayer meeting? What are you doing?"

"I already heard the Lord. I have to do my part." With that, he started to dig. He missed dinner that night and the prayer meeting too.

"I'm communing with the Lord right here," he said to his wife when she came out looking for him to go to prayer.

"Such a big field. Why are you digging here?"

"I'm not sure. But I figure the water will be right where it was when it disappeared, right here."

He dug far after sunset. In fact, he had to get the ladder from the hayloft so he could climb out of the hole. It was that deep.

The farmer's son came out before bedtime to see his dad still digging by the light of several lanterns.

"I figure the water will be right where it was when it disappeared, right here."

"What are you digging for, anyway?"

The boy did not understand when his father responded simply, "Rain, boy, I'm digging for rain."

"Dad, you are digging for rain?"

"You're the one who said it was here, boy. The spring rain, it's in here somewhere."

Immediately his understood. "Well, can I help?"

The farmer stopped for a moment, leaning on his shovel. The sweat dripped from his brow. The light of the lantern shined dimly on the man's face.

"You want to help find last spring's rain? Folks will think you're as crazy as me." A smile broke on his face as he looked toward his son.

"I sure do, Dad."

"Well, don't just stand there then, jump in this hole. God knows what your mother will say if..."

"She'll say it's fine, Dad. She will." The boy stopped long enough to embrace his father. I love you, Dad. We're in this together."

The farmer stretched his neck out of the hole a bit to see his wife looking out the window.

"The prayer meeting's over, but she hasn't stopped praying." He said half to himself.

Strengthened by the prayers of his wife and the confidence of his son, the farmer dug. With renewed hope. They dug together until the water began to spring up like a geyser. They scurried up the ladder as the hole quickly filled with water and began pouring over the field.

"Whoa! We got the rain, even when it isn't raining," the farmer shouted as he stood by the newly dug well, watching the life-giving waters flow into the parched soil and ultimately save the harvest. His son ran to the house shouting for his mom to come and see. The farmer took off his sweat-drenched hat and wiped his brow. He looked into the heavens with a smile. "Thank You for the river, Lord," he said and then followed his son to the house.

The River Always Flows

The old farmer had a revelation that saved his crop. The Lord had preserved the spring rain within the earth, just as He preserves the outpouring of His Spirit deep within our own hearts.

It is there, exactly where we left it so many years ago, for whatever reason. It matters not. It only matters that it is there, right where we saw it and experienced it last. To be sure, we never want to live in the past, but sometimes we must begin where we experienced Him last, in order to go on.

Many can feel the rumbling, flowing, almost burning sensation of His Presence, just waiting to spring up from within. The former rain—the spring rain—waters the earth as it falls, then goes underground and is preserved for later use. We just have to know where it is and how to get to it.

The spring rains are exactly where God planted Himself in us when we first believed. If we have the courage to dig through our guilt, our fear, and our condemnation, receiving God's forgiveness, we will find the refreshing river of God that flows so wonderfully within.

This river never runs dry, with or without our revival meetings.

For the river runs through us with its own force and its own power. It has a mind of its own. It does not need to be pumped or piped. It only needs an outlet—our willingness to say "yes" and to keep saying "yes."

The River and the Rain

Neither the former rain nor the latter rain alone is sufficient to bring the fields to the point where they are white for harvest. Both are needed. In fact, according to the prophet Joel, we need the spring rain twice. First in the spring and then again at the time of harvest, with the latter rain.

The latter rain comes from the clouds at the time of harvest. The early spring rains come from the earth at the time of harvest. The River of God's Presence is the river of God inside, and it is always flowing. It doesn't really matter whether it's raining or not. The river is there because of the spring rain and is flowing within. This river flows through me all summer to the time of the latter, harvest rain.

The former and the latter rain come together in those who release the river within and pray for the rain of the harvest.

Since we have His Presence with us, it is always oozing from us like an artesian well. Our lips can always flow with milk and honey to nourish a dying planet. For this flow is not dependent upon my mood or my attitude. It does not hinge upon whether I remembered to do all the "right" things. The river within is not dependent upon me, it flows because it has a life and destiny of its own. I have become a living prayer before the Lord to the nations, always open, always ready to hear, always ready to obey.

The Battle is Over

I am done battling the air for control of space that is relegated to the enemy. We have a High Priest, Christ Jesus our Lord, who has passed through the heavens. He can open the heavens anytime He wants. He won the war, not just the battle.

The air is not our dominion, for the enemy is the prince and power of the air. But the earth is the Lord's and all it contains. The enemy can clog up the heavens all he wants. I have a river that flows from the deepest part of my heart over which he has no control. At the right time, our Father will pour out the rain and it will unite with the river within. Oh, can you only imagine the Presence and mercy that will pour over the earth when the former and the latter rains meet within our hearts?

My war is over. I let the River of God within me flow through me to the nations. I no longer battle for a realm that the Lord will hand to us in due season.

When rain is not falling from the heavens, listen closely: You can hear the sound of a flowing river...within.

The secret is simple but profound.

The rain is always there, either from heaven or from within.

Chapter 7 Scripture References

Romans 12:2 PEB
II Corinthians 1:24 NKJV
Galatians 4:7 PEB
Matthew 16:19 NKJV
Colossians 1:18 PEB
Romans 12:1 NKJV

Colossians 3:1 PEB
I John 2:17 PEB
Matthew 17:20 PEB
Matthew 16:18 NKJV
Romans 12:4 PEB

Because of the River within me, I have become a living prayer before the Lord to the nations, always open, always ready to hear, always ready to obey.

*He is
putting an
unexplainable,
undefinable
devotion
to Him
into my
heart.*

CHAPTER 8

The Secret of Passion

Why is it that God put such a craving inside of us for Himself? It has to be He who has done it. Who else would want us to get so close to our Creator and lover? Certainly, it is not the enemy of our souls who gives us this relentless desire to see Him, to be one with Him. Certainly it is not our fleshy appetite that craves His Presence and is willing to lay anything aside for the sake of Him. Nor can it be said that we are a fluke of nature to desire Him more than even life itself. For even nature groans in pain, as though in the travail of childbirth, just waiting, anticipating, longing for His appearing.

Yes, it can clearly be said it is God who is gathering to Himself those who will come, those who will say "yes." He is putting into our hearts an indefinable and unexplainable devotion to Him. He does not respect the denominational walls built by men. He does not respect the doctrines developed by theologians more academic than spiritual. He does not even respect the traditions we thought so important over the years. He is blowing the wind of His Spirit into the hearts of those who have abandoned themselves to Him with utmost trust, having raised the sail of their spirit into the wind of God, which will ever blow us into Himself.

Without asking questions, without requiring explanation, we are saying "yes" to Him over and over again. Every time we feel the gentle tugging of His Presence within, our response is joyful anticipation of His desire.

There is a deep determination to never again fall short of His glory. We have been content with this for far too long. We have listened to the words of those who should have known better. We have sacrificed a relationship with the most intimate of lovers and believed another rather than respond to that for which our heart yearns.

But those days are mercifully gone. His nearness comforts us. His mercy draws us. His grace compels to us where He alone teaches and He alone fulfills the craving of the soul.

Sin Does Not Disqualify Us

Yes, it is true that we have sinned, but that sin does not disqualify us from His glory.

Our sin does not separate us from His Presence.

His blood is greater than our sin.

His glory is greater than our sin.

Forgiveness is greater than our sin.

It is impossible to imagine a sin committed by a hungry believer that could separate him from the Lord who gave Himself on our behalf. Our sin cannot be stronger than His blood.

Who Can Separate Us from Him?

So we sing songs about coming into His Presence. We read Scriptures about coming into His Presence. We want more than anything in the world to come into His Presence. But we don't, or we can't. What we have been taught and what we have believed holds us away from Him. So we live in frustration and emptiness. We live in fear without fulfillment or inner, personal satisfaction.

It has been enough to make a holy man fall away,

or a hungry man starve to death,

or the passionate person ultimately give up.

An argument with religion can never be won. Religion requires intellectual ascent for it dwells in natural realm. The reality of His Manifest Presence requires childlike faith. It dwells in the dimension of the unseen. The great eternity of God is where nothing is as it seems according to the rules that govern the natural dimension.

So, how long are we going to believe what dead men believed and taught so long ago? How long will we deny the longing of our souls, the tug of the Lord to a greater reality? How long will we ignore the inner witness of our hearts for the sake of what others probably have never experienced and certainly never understood?

Do we keep accepting these old doctrines without requiring the same test of doctrinal authenticity that we are required to undergo by them for our experience? How long can we deny the fruit that we ourselves bear as we love and respond to our Lord? Who will require of those who speak so eloquently of law and judgment and theology, the same measure of fruitful understanding of mercy, grace, and compassion?

How long will we ignore the inner witness of our hearts for the sake of what others probably have never experienced and certainly never understood?

Who will have the courage to respond to the Spirit of the Lord within, regardless of the consequences without? At what point will we come to understand that the traditions of man will never bring the glory of God? When will someone stand up and declare that the rules of the religious cannot condemn the relationship of the righteous?

Religion will always kill, steal, and destroy while the Lord will always forgive, heal, and restore to wholeness. I know, if no one else knows, that He is my only hope. Of course, we will always fail the test of the religious right, who are better at wielding the rule of law than the rule of grace.

The Spirit of the Lord Jesus within is poised to move upon us and on behalf of those who will believe the work of the Father in their hearts. This is not a prophecy. It is a fact. It is the posture of the Lord toward His people at any given moment in any given generation. He is forever poised to respond to anyone who will say 'yes' to Him. These have the courage to trust the Lord deep within them before they will believe the legalistic regulations of the religious system.

Courage is rising in His people.

Desperation is overwhelming fear.

Desire is beginning to rule in the hearts of those who love Him with love undying.

Today, if you hear His voice, do not harden your hearts. The great I AM whom we serve is suddenly appearing in His temple.

With a resounding "yes," the heavens and the earth are shaken by a bride who will no longer be denied her first love, her last love, her only love.

Chapter 8 Scripture References

Hebrews 12:11 NAS
II Corinthians 5:17 PEB
Matthew 9:17 PEB
Ephesians 4:11 PEB
Luke 1:37 PEB
Matthew 22:39 PEB
James 1:3 NAS

Romans 8:19 NKJV
Psalms 140:13 NKJV
Colossians 1:5 PEB
Ephesians 4:12 PEB
Isaiah 40:31 NKJV
III John 2 NKJV

The great I AM whom we serve is suddenly appearing in His temple.

God yearns
for the
permanent
restoration
of His
Presence
in my
heart.

CHAPTER 9

The Secret of Revival

The cold night air swept under the heavy oak doors. The old man shivered as he walked down the center aisle toward the foyer. The lights flickered with each gust of the wind. He stopped to pull his sweater around his waist, buttoning it with shaking hands. He wasn't sure why his hands shook the way they did. Maybe it was just the cold. Maybe it was his age. Maybe it was his sense of loss. But whatever caused his old hands to shake, it didn't much matter. The work had to be done and there was no one else who could do it or who cared to do it. He pulled an old knit hat out of his back pocket and brought it down over his ears.

He could almost see the chill pouring in through the crack under the door. "Meant to fix that," he muttered to himself as he pushed the broom to a pile of dust and lint already gathered from the other aisles. The lint moved across the floor with the wind like so many church mice entertaining themselves after a late service. But there was no late service. There was not an early service. Fact is, there was hardly ever a service here at all anymore. He looked quickly at his watch. It was close to eight o'clock, quitting time.

He finished the floor, gathered his things, and began walking slowly to the back door. The wheels of the trash bin screeched, echoing through the hall. He stopped to look around as the sound bounced from wall to wall, as though it did not want to end.

The old hall was used to sound, a lot of sound.

He fought the urge to allow memories of the old days to well up again. He couldn't bear to rehearse the worship, the preaching, and the repentance that had happened here in the Presence of God.

As he walked down the center aisle, still pulling the old trash bin, he could still sense the Presence, as though waiting for another meeting, another song, another heart.

"There will be no more meetings like that, at least not anytime soon. There will be no more preaching like that," the old man thought to himself. Then, smiling, his thoughts went another direction: "Except for the times I go to the podium." He loved preaching, imagining the place was full of hungry and hopeful hearts, all eager to hear the Word. He never preached for real. No one knew the times he timidly walked to the podium when the place was empty. He loved to hear the words that always broke his heart and always caused him to melt in His Presence. But it was over. Revival was over. God had stopped moving. The Lord had decided, or so they always said, that the time of visitation was over.

He never really bought that. To him, God loved the fellowship of the saints and yearned to dwell in the praises of His people.

Anyway, who would listen to him? He pushed the trash bin out the door, turned to lock the dead bolt, and started home. But as he walked away, he turned as he sensed a yearning, a desire from inside the hall.

The old man's eyes filled with tears as his heart burned and his spirit leaped at the feeling that God was still there, still waiting for someone, anyone, to respond.

"Yep," he said to himself, "the only ones who decided the visitation was over was us." He stood for a long moment staring at that old oak door and feeling the fire in his heart. With a deep breath he turned away and started the long walk home.

Why is Revival Over?

How many times in history has this scene, or scenes just like it, been repeated? How many times have we been in the position of trying to explain why revival seemed to end as the Presence of God vanished from common experience?

The question is rather simple. It's the answers we don't want to consider.

Shall we do what we have done with so many other things in the Church? Shall we develop a doctrine to explain why we do not experience the Presence as a sustained occurrence among us?

That might satisfy the intellect. It might satisfy the religious among us. But it will not satisfy the yearning hunger in the hearts of so many people who do not want excuses. They want His Presence.

It does not satisfy the heart of God, who has dreamed a dream for us that will not be satisfied by explaining away why God doesn't show Himself as He did in the past.

Is revival something that happens in the building and not in the heart? When revival "leaves" a church building, does that mean His Presence leaves our experience? If we have the Presence as a sustained experience in our lives, will His Presence ever seem to diminish over time in meetings?

'Revival' begins when God says things we want to hear. Revival ends when God begins to say things we do not want to hear.

Truth is, God is not as finicky as we make Him out to be. Mysterious? Yes. Hard to find? No.

He is not a collection of dos and don'ts. Relationship with Him is not found in the sum of so many activities that we believe will bring favor to the doer.

'Revival' begins when God says things we want to hear. Revival ends when God begins to say things we do not want to hear.

From His perspective, He is not interested in 'revival'. God wants the permanent restoration of His Presence in the lives of those who make up the Church, the Body of Christ on earth. He will only be content with "Emmanuel," God with us in the sustained sense of His Presence in our lives.

But we have had to come up with good believable reasons why God seems to move in seasons or temporary visitations. There has to be a way to explain why we never seem to experience the lasting manifest Presence of the Lord either in our lives or in the Church. It cannot possibly be our fault. It is always just the timing of God, isn't it?

When we pray for 'revival', we are praying for the Presence of the Lord to be manifest among us. We all know that God is omnipresent. He is everywhere. But omnipresence is not Manifest Presence. That is, His Presence is detectable by one or more of the five natural senses. His Presence is manifest when He can be sensed in the dimension of time and space. The cry of the Church that Jesus is building today is the cry for His Manifest Presence.

While praying for revival, we often find ourselves repenting of things we are glad to give up. You know what those kinds of things are. They haunt us and tempt us and can rather easily cause us to fall into sin. These things distract us from devotion to the Lord and the dream He has dreamed for us The dream he has put into our hands whether preaching to the masses or tenderly raising our children in the love and admonition of the Lord is what will bring a long-term sense of fulfillment.

In His gentle and predictable mercy, God shows Himself to us and delivers us from the sin that so easily besets us. He forgives us. Guilt is gone and hope is restored to our hearts. The weight of a thousand sorrows lifts from us.

Revival Begins.

We bask in the wonder and freedom of His forgiveness. We are truly like those who dream of such liberty but never experience it. Naturally, our joy and freedom overflow into the lives of those who are close to us. Soon we are leading others into the same experience we are enjoying.

Revival Grows.

We are caught up in the power of the experience. In the ecstasy of the moment, we forget that we are on a journey. We lose sight that He is at work within us to conform us to His image. We do not remember that we are at the beginning of something wonderfully supernatural and not at the end. We forget that in the awe of the moment, we have asked Him to change us, prepare us, and use us. In response to the requests we have made over the years, He begins to show us the things that still hide deep within that will most certainly hinder us from the dream He has dreamed for us.

But we really did not expect Him to answer those prayers of dedication and consecration. In fact, if the truth be known, we thought those prayers were easy to pray because we did not imagine anything else lurked inside of us that would battle against His Presence and His purpose for us.

But those things are there. He is finding things we are not willing to give to Him.

He may be urging you to forgive someone who does not deserve to be forgiven. He may be showing you something that you refuse to believe is hidden deep in you heart. The Holy Spirit is hindered by stubbornness and unbelief once again. We have forgotten the joy and wonder of living in the 'yes' of God. His Presence seems to wane.

Soon, we grow tired of the work of revival.

His Presence has lost its wonder.

Revival Ends.

"The visitation is over," we lament in our hearts.

"Wasn't it wonderful?"

For you see, 'revival' is never the real issue. Times of refreshing will come and go through the ages.

He is not interested in revival as we define it.

He is passionate for the permanent restoration of His Presence in the Church, in us, in me.

Chapter 9 Scripture References

Psalms 140:13 NAS
Matthew 11:28-30 PEB
Colossians 1:24 NKJV
Romans 10:9-10 NKJV
Matthew 6:14 PEB

Matthew 5:6 PEB
Luke 24:32 PEB
Revelation 21:6 PEB
Hebrews 11:1 PEB

The dream he has put into our hands whether preaching to the masses or tenderly raising our children in the love and admonition of the Lord is what will bring a long-term sense of fulfillment.

He
*is my only
desire,
my one
true
love.*

CHAPTER 10

The Secret of His Abiding Presence

The early morning haze rose lazily over the cornfields as Cathy and I walked back toward our home. The first rays of the sun warmed our backs, chasing away the chill of the dawn.

The Saturday morning ritual was about to begin. The smell of sizzling bacon would reach five tiny noses as they slept. Soon, starving boys would run down the stairs and into the kitchen, wiping their eyes and yawning like they needed more sleep. They probably did.

Cathy organized the labor force as they appeared in front of the stove, hoping for something to munch on. One started with the bagels and English muffins. Two set the table. The last two emptied the refrigerator of everything that could possibly be consumed at breakfast. Eggs, pancakes, French toast—the Saturday morning feast was truly a sight to behold. The noise and laughter was always a great start for the day. As the years passed, it would become a wonderful memory.

As we returned to the house on this particular Saturday morning, we noticed a small face pressed against the picture window of the living room. His big brown Italian eyes seemed to take up most of his face. But today those eyes were moist with tears. As we walked through the door, he jumped into his mother's arms with a predictable question.

"When are Grammy and Granddad going to be here? I've been waiting for them all morning."

"Donald, they are probably still in bed. I don't think they are going to be here until lunchtime."

With a big sigh, he walked back to the window. "I think I'll just wait here until they come."

We laughed. "Tell you what, Donald, come with me to the kitchen and you can break all the eggs for breakfast," his mother said.

A smile streaked across his face. Mom knew that no little boy would be able to resist the chance to break eggs.

Soon the tumult of breakfast was over and the kitchen, now a wasted, howling wilderness after five boys were finished, was abandoned for baseball, bikes, and tree houses.

Except for Donald.

He dutifully returned to his post at the living room window, waiting for Grammy and Granddad. He sat there for three hours, jumping every time a car drove past the lane. But as Mom had predicted, they arrived just before noon. It is hard to describe the scene of dirty little boys running and shouting for joy with the arrival of their grandparents. Hugs, kisses, smiles, and laughter made an unforgettable, albeit noisy, welcoming committee.

The afternoon went by quickly with stories and games and a nap for Granddad. Although they had to give up their playroom while he slept, the boys were happy to do it for their best friend. But it was a little harder for the boys when their playroom-turned-bedroom had to be vacated far earlier than they expected.

"Mom, but it's so early."

"It's just for the weekend. You can survive for a few nights."

"A few nights! They're staying a few nights? I don't want to give up the playroom for a few nights!"

"Yes, you all knew they were staying until Monday. It will be fine. Think of all the fun you are having."

Somehow, the fun they were missing was beginning to outweigh the fun they were having. But the playroom was not all that caused problems. Sunday morning had to be very quiet until Grammy and Granddad got up. Lunch was at a restaurant instead of their favorite hamburger shop. They all had to go to a concert in the afternoon, and they still could not get into their playroom. Life had quickly become so frustrating, and all because their favorite people had come to visit.

Sunday evening, as we sat in the living room with my parents, I saw a small face pressed against the picture window. Donald was looking in the window with his large brown eyes filled with tears. I excused myself and walked out to the porch.

Donald threw his arms around me and asked a predictable question. "When are Grammy and Granddad leaving?"

It is a good thing that Grammy and Granddad came to visit and not to stay. This happy household would certainly have turned into a most unhappy place to live.

A visitation from the Lord is just like this weekend with the grandparents. We never plan for a visitation from God to turn into anything permanent. That's probably why visitation is just that—a visitation. It's easy to say that He comes for a season and then, for whatever sovereign reason deep in God's heart, He leaves. But God never intended to visit us. He has always planned to stay. It is

If you only want a visitation, then plan for a visitation.

only our man-made doctrines of visitation that justify the fact that the Presence of God does not abide among us.

So here is the secret. If you only want a visitation, then plan for a visitation. But if you hunger for the permanent restoration of God's Manifest Presence among His people, plan for Him to stay. Prepare for Him. Expect Him. Welcome Him. Yield to Him. Continuously make room in your heart for Him. He will come. He will come to stay.

Chapter 10 Scripture References

John 14:2,3   Matthew 1:23

Prepare for Him. Expect Him. Welcome Him. Yield to Him.

I am
only visiting
this planet.
I will follow
the Son,
wherever
He will
lead me.

CHAPTER 11

The Secret of Moving On with God

It was an incredible sight. Huge campfires dotted the landscape in the blackness of the night. People were coming out of the darkness in large numbers, gathering around one fire or another. Those who tended the fires worked feverishly to keep the flames climbing into the darkness. There seemed to be no end to the fire or to the people who rushed with great joy from the darkness of the night.

Occasionally, a log was taken from an existing fire and carried triumphantly to an area of darkness where a new fire was started. Grand celebrations were easily recognizable as more and more people came to the new fire.

Soon, groups of people who had come out of the darkness moved from fire to fire, enjoying the unique experience. More and more people gathered. The leaders were clearly thrilled at the effect of the fires on the people. They became more and more confident that their fires were sure to be a center of life for the weary sojourner for many years to come.

But just when the celebration seemed to peak, something very strange and quite unexpected happened. It occurred quite subtly at first, with nearly everyone remaining oblivious to what was slowly appearing on the eastern horizon. A thin strip of light had cut across the darkened landscape. Some took notice, however, and began moving in great wonder and amazement toward this brightness. Quickly this thin strip of light grew until a slice of brilliant orange rose above the horizon. More people took notice. The brightness of the fires seemed to dim, although they roared with the same intensity as before. Soon, the rising of the Son overtook the valley. Without a moment of hesitation, people began moving away from the fires and walked toward the rising Son.

Most of the leaders became anxious. The light of their fires, once the only beacon throughout the dismal and hopeless night, faded in the emergent Son light. In a desperate attempt to save the fires and the hope they offered, the leaders commanded more firewood for the fires. But it was to no avail. The people continued to move away from the fires, not because they were not good in the desperation of the night, but now...but now...something they had waited for all their lives was coming. Now, a substitute would not do, for the Son was rising.

The leaders frantically searched for logs to add to their waning fires. The bonfires that once burned brilliantly in the night now struggled to be seen beyond their own gathering of people. Someone determined that this drawing away of the people was the work of an enemy. A great council was called to study the probable threat and to discern what needed to be done to revive the revival. They quickly decided to combine the bonfires. Yes, it was most definitely time for a true show of unity. The people appeared to be running helter-skelter, while the fires were orderly and controllable.

The remaining fuel was gathered and shared in order to make the flames burn as brightly as possible. But the flames could not and would not ever overcome the rising of the Son in the land. Soon, even many of those who tended the fires began to run toward the Son's rising. The abandoned fires lost their strength. They were no longer being carefully tended and had no sustaining life within themselves.

As more and more people recognized the Son, they abandoned everything to run to Him. They were listening to their hearts. They were responding to their passion. With shouts of joy and anticipation they allowed themselves to give in to Him. This is what their hearts had always yearned for. They were not going to turn away from Him, no matter the cost to their reputations.

People left everything or nearly everything behind. Nothing else was important to them now. Like a crowd running from a burning building, they ignored the warnings and threats of the few who still tended the dying fires of what was passing away. Most fires were now nothing more than piles of smoldering coals smoking in the early morning light. Folks ran past them and sometimes through them as they responded to the love in their hearts.

The Son was rising. The Son was pouring His warmth, His light, His peace over the darkness. Now the people were seeing like they had never seen before.

Some leaders, being committed to His Kingdom instead of their own, welcomed the Son with great joy and relief. The Lord had come in all His glory. The message of preparation and the intercessory prayer toward the Lord and His manifest Presence had been answered. Now the people would find Him in His majesty and mercy. They were glad to decrease as the Lord increased in their midst. They were eager to yield to Him, eager to give Him the pre-eminence they had promised He would have when He appeared among them. Now He would be the center of attention. Now the people would rely on Him instead of mere humans. Now they would flee to Him for all they needed. He would be their testimony. The people would begin gathering others to the Lord and not to a meeting. Now His Kingdom would be established in the hearts of men, not in an individual church or organization.

But others were merely frightened men waving burning sticks and shouting slanderous accusations at those who had discovered the love for which they had yearned over the years.

These leaders were just like Paul. He thought he was so important to the work of God as he persecuted believers, chasing them down from city to city. He was certain he was doing the right thing until the light of heaven knocked him off his horse. That is when Paul's light was turned to utter darkness. How small Paul's light really was compared to the brightness of

His glory! Men's campfires only seem awesome until compared with the brightness of the Son.

But they were too consumed with their own value to understand the significance of the rising of the Son. These guys were to be pitied. For the Son was rising upon them as well. The Son was pouring His hope in their lives too. But, alas, they were too concerned about the fading importance of their own kingdoms. They were too concerned about their place in the system, in history.

How easy it would have been to simply pursue the Son. How renewing it could have been for them to allow the Lord to give them a brand new wineskin, a new heart, a new desire, a new hope for the future. How powerful it would have been to find their Lord in a new and deeper way, hearing His voice and moving by His Spirit as in the days of old.

To be sure, many people fought the urge deep in their hearts to go to the Son, choosing instead to be part of the last and fading memory of a smoldering system that had served its purpose. These folks frantically gathered the ashes in a heap—one last monument to those who valued the position of man before the purpose of God.

Now their gatherings were gatherings around the light of His Manifest Presence and not the light of human effort and religious tradition, even if it was new tradition.

But the Son continued to rise. People gathered again to talk of the Lord and marvel over the mercy and love of God. But their gatherings this time were much different. Now their gatherings were gatherings around the light of His Manifest Presence and not the light of human effort and religious tradition, even if it was new tradition. In these new gatherings, He was the focus, He was the sum, and He was the substance. Nothing else mattered, and nothing else was important. His people were consumed in the awe of His Life and His Presence. These desperate believers finally got it. They were looking to the man-made fires of religion for hope and fulfillment. But they made a startling discovery. They discovered that the fires of God burned within them, if they only took the time to search in the one place they had never thought to find Him—in the throne room of their own hearts.

History is blaring with the lesson of the Son. When the Son shines, we must move with Him. The arguments of those who choose to resist the Son's appearing fade in His glory as He fills open and hungry hearts afresh with the hope of His Presence.

History resonates with the unmistakable fruit of those who have either resisted or followed the Son.

Time is littered with the sweaty efforts of man and his meager attempts to keep ablaze a fire that God has long since abandoned. What begins in the Spirit will most certainly end in the flesh if we are not willing to move as He moves. When our testimonies become dated and our worship songs become instrumental meditations, we should recognize that we have long since abandoned the fire of the Spirit for the safer and more predictable services of a religious system that has no future and no life within itself.

The sojourn comes to a bitter end when we are more concerned with our appearance before man than our obedience before the Living God. No longer are we led by the song of the Lord or the sweet melodies of prophetic encouragement. No longer do we leap at the sound of His voice or pant at the call of our name in the quiet of our prayer closet. The fire is built. The lot is paved, and our spirits have become very much like them, hard and impenetrable. They are permanently fixed in the system and in history. They are good only as they recognize the ones He will use in our place. We announce their arrival on the scene by our voices of condemnation and ridicule toward hearts soft and pliable as ours once were.

The King is Coming—In Me

We are only visiting this planet. We are sojourning in this land of time and space and flesh and blood. His Kingdom is coming. The permanent restoration of the King's Presence in the earth, in us, in me is the hope we long for. It is the solution we have believed for. It brings rest to the weary heart and health to those who love Him with love undying. He carries true destiny into the hearts of His own and fulfillment to all who have hoped in His appearing.

We will build no monuments, no towers. We will keep our hearts open and our spirits unfurled like a sail of ship, waiting for the wind of God to take us to our next adventure. For the wind blows where it will. We hear the sound of it, but we do not know where it has come from or where it is going. So is everyone who is born of His Spirit. But our bags are packed and we are ready to respond to His voice, wherever He may lead.

This is the secret of moving on with God.

Chapter 11 Scripture References

II Chronicles 19:11 NKJV
Luke 2:20 PEB
John 1:32-34 PEB
Matthew 10:32-33 PEB
I Peter 1:21 NAS

Luke 1:31-33 PEB
Luke 2:40 PEB
Galatians 2:20 NKJV
Philemon 21 NAS

In these new gatherings, He was the focus, He was the sum, and He was the substance. Nothing else mattered, and nothing else was important.

The
name of
Jesus
is not
a magic
word.

CHAPTER 12

The Secret of Jesus' Name

"Again I say to you, that if two of you agree on earth about anything that they may ask, it shall be done for them by My Father who is in heaven. For where two or three have gathered together in My name, there I am in their midst." Matt. 18: 19-20

"Truly, truly, I say to you, he who believes in Me, the works that I do shall he do also; and greater works than these shall he do; because I go to the Father. And whatever you ask in My name, that will I do, that the Father may be glorified in the Son. If you ask Me anything in My name, I will do it." Jn.14:12-14

The Name of Jesus is Not a Magic Word.

The utterance of His name in prayer is a solemn witness and a determined testimony to every authority and power in the heavens and on the earth that the King has determined something and it will most surely come to pass. It puts humanity and the spirit world on notice that there is a will greater than theirs; there is a power greater than theirs.

Further, it declares that there are some in this dimension who not only believe it but also will announce it in confidence and complete assurance that the will of the King is about to be done. His will is about to be accomplished in spite of the ranting of demon forces, and the unbelief of nay sayers. A believer's prayer in time and space is a completed circuit that begins in the heart of God and is fulfilled with the faith of man. The Word becomes flesh when man has heard from the King and pronounces it on earth. This completed circuit releases the power of heaven and the angels to accomplish the decree of the King.

The name of Jesus is not a magic word.

His name is uttered with reverence and divine fear. For when a man prays in His most powerful Name, he is declaring that he has heard from the King and is carrying that message to its fulfillment. He is certain that God will answer for he has labored in prayer before the King and heard His voice. Therefore God will bring it to pass.

The fulfillment of our random, sometimes wanton desires was never the intention of the Lord. For when He spoke to His disciples, He knew they would hear His voice and they would believe Him. "Don't be afraid to ask anything, in My name," He assured His disciples. "I will do what you are hearing in your spirit. I AM talking to you."

The name of Jesus is not a magic word.

A few years ago, several of us were in intercessory prayer seeking the direction of the Lord in our work. Suddenly the Spirit of the Lord began to speak from deep within. He spoke to one of us that a few needed to go to a certain country for a very specific purpose. In amazement, two other people were hearing that precise word from the Lord. Three of us agreed that we had touched God's heart in the matter. We were confident it was the Lord's will since it was witnessed among us, independently and sovereignly. As we responded in faith, there was a wonderfully supernatural result.

Sometimes the ego of man finds it so difficult to see the Body of Christ. Many things have been done in the name of Jesus that were merely born out of the desire of one person. Many are more concerned with their personal plans than they are with the will of God. In our situation, had there not been a witness among us, there would not have been the needed confirmation to be confident that the Lord was truly speaking. The trip would not have been made.

The name of Jesus is not a magic word.

You Shall Know Them by Their Fruit

If our traditional understanding of these verses is true, why do we not see the results of so many prayers we have prayed in this fashion?

Why is it that we do not have the job, the spouse, the car, the house, the clothes, the ministry that we have asked for in this fashion?

We have taken these verses so selfishly. For we have believed that if we simply agree on anything we want, He will provide it for us. But in the Most Holy Place, He is the center of activity. He is the beginning and the end of everything.

This is the realm of all-God.

The people who serve Him there have voluntarily relinquished their own rights and become bondservants of a higher mission in another dimension called eternity. It is in this realm that we understand we are possessed and controlled by a King who does not get His authority from this dimension or the people of this dimension. He does not need the permission or the protection of a failing religious system to complete His will in the earth.

Orders from the King

Prayer is our response to the orders and desires of our King. Prayer is our agreement with His plan. Prayer is not an attempt to convince Him to do what we want done. The whiny, fleshy prayers of a carnal church do not move God nor do they plant His Life and Kingdom on the earth.

Remember the words of Jesus:

"I only do what I see my Father in Heaven doing."

"If it be possible, let this cup pass from me. Nevertheless, not my will, but your will be done."

These are not the prayers of a self-centered church trying to get whatever they want.

The name of Jesus is not a magic word.

Heaven does not Need to be Stormed.

Many prayers are hollow and empty because they are not prayers at all. They are our own hopes and desires that we are passing off as the decree of the King, except they are spoken without the authority of the King. This authority can only come from those who genuinely hear from the King on a specific matter. Otherwise, no one is moved by them, certainly not God.

Some insist that prayers and Scripture verses need to be repeated again and again. It is thought that we need to claim what we want and storm heaven's gates. But the King is easy to be heard. He is decreeing health, restoration, salvation, and wisdom all the time. If we will simply grow quiet in our spirit, we will hear His decree about the matter for which we seek Him. Then we can shout it from the housetops, not to get His attention but because He has gotten our attention and we are certain of what He has said to us.

When we pray, it is because we have heard the voice of the King. We know that a particular matter will come to pass because we have heard it from the King Himself. We have long abandoned the concocted prayers based on our own reason and intellect. Now we only respond to the word of the Lord. Even when it defies reason, we choose to believe Him.

Genuine Kingdom Theology

Jesus taught us to pray for His Kingdom to come here and now, on this planet, in this and every generation, in our hearts, in good times and in bad. We fully expect the rule and reign of Jesus to be established in the earth, beginning with us.

From the beginning of time, it was His plan to redeem for Himself a people for His own possession, a people after His own heart, who are committed to the will of God rather than the will of mere mortal men.

It is much easier to pray "Thy Kingdom come" when we are praying for the world. The prayer is broad enough that our personal life does not seem to be affected. But when we pray "Thy Kingdom come in me" we are praying a much different prayer. For now we are asking God to plant His Kingdom seed in us. We are asking Him to use whatever means possible to bring His dream about in our own life, personally.

"Thy Kingdom come" is comfortably prayed by folks all over the world. But it is prayed without the understanding that God's Kingdom does not come as the kingdoms of men come and go. God is not looking for territories or land masses. He does not draw geopolitical boundaries when He establishes His rule and reign on the earth.

His Kingdom is first established in much more difficult and hostile terrain. His Kingdom first must come in the human heart.

His Kingdom is first established in much more difficult and hostile terrain. His Kingdom first must come in the human heart. It is established one person at a time. One confession at a time. Our Lord works out the hardness of our hearts, plants the seed of His love, and then proceeds to remove those things that will most certainly hinder the growth of the seed He has planted.

His rule is secured in the hearts of people just like you and me. His Kingdom is not marked by boundaries as human kingdoms are marked. His Kingdom crosses every border and can be found in every land and language.

Hearing the Voice of the King

The King is the only One who teaches us what to do and what to say. He alone gives us permission to speak in His Name, when, of course, we have yielded to Him who rules within and we have heard the sound of His voice.

He knows what He wants to do and what He wants to accomplish. He knows what He wants to say and who He wants to say it to. He needs neither our advice nor our wisdom. He needs our hearts, our voices, and our willingness to allow Him to do His will through us.

One of the hardest things for humanity to do is to trust Him. But we love to pollute the spiritual atmosphere with our fleshy prayers. The human side of us whines for our own wants and personal desires. But these prayers only create smog in the spiritual atmosphere and prevent the Lord from doing what is best for us.

"Thy Kingdom come" is a prayer totally devoid of our own, sometimes whining desires. It is like a cold wind blowing over the land. It clears away the dust and smoke of our selfish desires and unbelief. It opens the way for the purpose of the Lord to be done, in us, through us, and around us.

Our prayers should release the power of Christ to have His way. In my heart of hearts, I can often hear the Lord praying through me. These prayers bring comfort, true exhilaration, and hope. I hear Him calling out to His Father, "Not My will, but Your will be done. I just want what You want." My heart joins Him with prayers like this. There is no question that the most God-moving prayer I can pray is for His will to be done in my life and in those around me.

In the past, when I have gone to the Lord in prayer, my prayers were somewhat different. The first ten minutes were usually spent in a counseling session. I wanted the Lord to understand what the problem was and what I wanted Him to do about it. Then I followed this counseling time with a plea for Him to accept my analysis of the situation. Then I asked Him to do what I had decided was the correct course of action.

His name cannot be used to invoke the power of God to do the will of man.

We clutter the air with prayers born out of frustration, fear, and uncertainty, as though He needs our wisdom and advice on how to deal with an issue. Then we pray all these things in the name of Jesus. We are certain that if we pray in the name of Jesus, He will do exactly what we want Him to do. After all, we *did* pray in His name.

But the name of Jesus is not a magic word.

His name cannot be used to invoke the power of God to do what we want.

Praying in the Name of Jesus

When you pray in the name of Jesus, you are praying in the name of the King. You are praying as a messenger of the will of the King. You are announcing something to the world, both natural and spiritual, that the King wants to happen.

Those who pray in the name of Jesus, the King, are like medieval criers who walked the highways of the kingdom announcing the will and intentions of the king who ruled the kingdom. "In the name of the king, vacate these premises, for the king will build a new castle here!"

Everyone believes the crier because he comes in the name of the king.

"In the name of the king, all subjects must be on the castle grounds for the coronation of the new queen. In the name of the king, all are expected to attend!"

The one who pronounces those words represents the king. He knows the will of the king and is announcing the king's will with authority and assurance. He is not coming with his own message, he is voicing the desire and intentions of the king.

"I come in the name of the king" is the testimony of the medieval crier.

For the most part, we live in the Holy Place, that is, the place of selfish desire and personal greed instead of the Most Holy Place, the realm of selfless surrender and the realm of all-God. In the Holy Place, our fantasies are in constant conflict with the will of the King, who will always put His plan above our own. For He knows that His plan will lead to life, peace, and personal fulfillment beyond our wildest imagination, but our selfish, fleshy plan will only leave us short of His glory.

The Holy Place is a place of personal struggle. It is where we develop our doctrines according to our own hidden desires. These personally contrived beliefs give us assurance that we will be certain to get what we want, at least among men. In the Holy Place, the will of man burgeons out of control, financed by weak and volatile believers who have no strength of discernment or wisdom within themselves. Of course, these Holy Place kingdom-builders count on ignorance to succeed. If true discernment broke out, they would be out of business in a moment of time.

Abide in the King's Presence

There is only one way the crier can come through town announcing with confidence in the name of the King. He must truly have been in the King's presence. He knows what he is supposed to say because he heard it from the King's lips for himself. Those who have heard the King for themselves will recognize His voice in the words of the crier, and they will be quick to respond to the message he brings them.

When you hear the voice of the King, you can announce His will with confidence.

The Lord awaits those who will hear His voice.

He has wonderful dreams to bring to pass—the dreams He has dreamed for you.

This is the secret to having every prayer you utter answered. Listen carefully to hear what our Lord is praying. Then join in His prayer to our heavenly Father, who is waiting for the prayers He will most certainly answer—His own.

Chapter 12 Scripture References

Psalms 4:1 NKJV

Romans 7:4 PEB

Matthew 28:18 PEB

Matthew 26:39 PEB

I Peter 1:18-21 NKJV

Proverbs 3:5 NAS

Philemon 1:9-10 NKJV

Psalms 20:4 NKJV

Revelations 21:6 PEB

Luke 2:49 PEB

Matthew 6:10 PEB

Ephesians 3:17 PEB

Romans 12:2 PEB

The name of Jesus is not a magic word.

*I refuse
to live
within the
boundaries
of the
status
quo.*

CHAPTER 13

The Secret of Balance

I hate balance.

There is nothing more boring than listening to a balanced person. He spends so much time building walls around what he says that he says nothing at all.

People who say they are balanced are too concerned about being acceptable.

I am not concerned about being acceptable.

My concern is yielding enough to the One who possesses me from within that He can do through me whatever He wants to do.

I hate balance.

Folks who are balanced never change the world. They never affect society. They live safely within the boundaries of the status quo, never challenging the forces that control society, the culture, or the church system. They believe that by reinforcing what is, they will encourage folks to move on. Fact is, balance is the bane of progress. It leads us to believe everything is as it should be, when in reality we are desperate for change, anxious to see and hear from the Lord concerning the things still locked in the heavens. Though the heavens are pregnant with His purposes and eternity dips into time and space, balanced folk explain away the restlessness within. Balanced folk redirect our focus to what has always been. They have the uncanny ability to make the hungry feel guilty for their hunger and the restless feel rebellious for their questions.

Balanced people are what everybody likes to have under their control. Balanced people don't ever rock the boat. But the Reformation never would have happened without imbalance. The Renaissance never would have happened without imbalance. The great revivals never would have happened without imbalance.

Imbalance is the key to our growth. It questions what we have done, why we are doing it, and where we are going.

An Adventure Waiting to Happen

Balance tries to convince us there is nothing new under the sun. When in fact everything is new under the sun. Balanced folk love to quote a frustrated and depressed old man who cries out in his depression, "There is nothing new under the sun!" But to our tiny masses of gray matter, everything is absolutely new. God may know everything, but I sure don't. For me, every day is an adventure waiting to happen. Every day is an irreplaceable opportunity to see, hear, and do things I have never even imagined could happen. Each day holds the possibility—no, the probability; no, the certainty—that the heavens will open above me and His Presence will flow within me creating an atmosphere of wonder and awe that will most certainly change me and the world around me.

Humans have always tried to re-box what God has un-boxed.

To be sure, there is nothing new to the Lord, but for us there are new mercies, new hopes, new possibilities opened to us every day—if we are unbalanced enough to be open to them.

God Talks to Us Out of the Box

God always talks to us outside the box we have constructed for ourselves. You know that box. It keeps you safe and assured that you are fine just as you are. Our nature is to always define circumstances, feelings, dreams, hopes, and possibilities within the parameters of what has always given us contentment. This box assures us that we are, well, balanced.

But this thought is not new. Humans have always tried to re-box what God has un-boxed. Jesus warned us not to put new wine into old wineskins.

Yes, the most boring person in the universe is a balanced person.

Church as We Know It, is Over

The true pastor must minister from two perspectives. He will always be a pastor, looking out for the well-being of the people. But he will also be open to the new things God will speak to the people, even if what God says is out of the pastor's experience. His concern is for the safety of the flock, but his concern is also for the Church coming into the dream God has dreamed for each individual. He understands that heaven is our destination, but it is not our destiny. The Lord will send many to him to train, equip, and send off to who-knows-where. Not everyone God sends to him is there to expand his ministry. Believers should mostly come to go. They come to be trained and go to fulfill their destiny. The pastor must be sure of who he is and where he is, without feeling threatened when God sends someone with a greater gift than his own. He must always be secure and free enough to equip, train, and then release.

He will most certainly have a base of permanent folks whose ministry it is to care for the needs and train those whom God sends. The Church becomes what God intended it to be, a school for the equipping of the saints for the work of the ministry. The five-fold ministry are not the ones that travel the world. They equip and send out those whom they have trained.

Spiritual Specialists?

Why is it that when doctors study a specified medical area they are called specialists, but when Christians give themselves to a specialized area they are called unbalanced? Doctors must rely on their relationships with other doctors whose specializations are different from their own, thereby having experts in areas they know little or nothing about. Specialists in the medical profession build relationships with other doctors whose opinions they not only trust, but rely upon. This is normal and expected practice. A doctor who tries to be individually thorough in his understanding of the intricate workings of the entire human body is ironically considered ineffective. He dismisses himself from the treasure of information and technique available to those who accept their own personal and professional limitations. The day of the general practitioner is quickly coming to an end.

The day of the church system's one-man-show is too.

God Sounds Outrageous

God speaks to us outside of our paragons. Everything He says to us sounds outrageous. Our tendency is to dismiss those things that are risky. But when we dismiss the outrageous, we too often dismiss God.

When God says something to us that we have never heard before, it often sounds exciting, even though it may bring fear to our hearts. Sometimes that fear turns to exhilaration at the thought of doing something so different. Subconsciously, however, we take a familiar course of action. In our minds, we visit all the people who are important to us to determine how they will react to this outrageous thing we have just heard. Once the votes are cast, most of the time we dismiss this outrageous, albeit exhilarating, thing we have heard, simply because most of the people we care about and who are important to us dismiss it. Even though we believe it, even though it made our heart sing and burn within us, we reject it because our friends have too.

That is why so many end up doing what has always been done. Too many people fear the outrageous. They fear anything that God says outside the box they have created for themselves, which, by the way, they have secretly learned to despise. We all like to think of ourselves as so open minded, so charismatic, so Spirit-filled, when in fact we have created a box in which everything we believe is locked. It keeps us balanced.

Balanced people never change the world.

They put you to sleep.

Balance is not in the person.

Balance is in the Body of Christ.

Go Fly a Kite

When I was a kid, I loved to fly kites. My mom would often say to my twin brother, Ron, and me, "Boys, why don't you guys go fly a kite." So we would. We spent hours in the golden meadows and fossil beds next to our rural Pennsylvania home.

A kite is an awesome thing. Even in a shallow wind, it is determined to fly. As the wind grows stronger, the kite's paper panels stretch out as it soars for the heavens, as though never to return.

Did you ever notice that a kite never seems to be content as it responds to the wind? As it pulls the string from the one holding it on the ground, the kite goes up as though on some secret mission. The kite has no concept that there is a limit as to how far the string will allow it to go. I was often the one holding the roll of string as the kite pulled away from us on its quest to go higher. The roll burned my fingers as we heard the whiz of the string chasing the kite heavenward. The wind often carried the kite until all the string was off the roll. We could barely see the kite, now only a dot against the sun-lit sky.

I always hated when I was out of string, for it created a dilemma. It is never the kite that limits its own flight. The string is always the bad guy. When the string was out, I either had to run with the kite or pull it back down. The kite usually pulled so hard that I feared for the kite. I never really was certain how much stress the string could take before it snapped. So I would run with the kite. I would run until there was some sort of danger. Power lines, a tree, another kite, a highway—all were hindrances to the kite's ability to soar with the wind or my ability to give it what it really wanted: more string.

All that kite wanted to do was fly, and there was no convincing it that imminent danger was ahead. The kite had captured the wind and wanted nothing more than to go with it, to yield to it, to go as far and as high and as fast as the wind dare take it. But when the string was gone, tension would mount and the exhilaration of the day quickly turned into stress as the battle to pull it back in ensued. I had to somehow work the string so as to gently bring the kite safely back to the ground. As many of you know, this is not an easy assignment. The kite is completely sold out to the wind and has no intentions of responding to someone earthbound and unable to experience the exhilaration of this kind of flight.

I can still almost hear the kite as it battled for its life: "What are you doing? I thought you loved to fly! Let me go!"

So the tension on the string grew as I called the kite back to earth. In my desire to give it string and yet protect it to fly another day, I found myself taking risks I would normally not take. I wanted it to soar on, but I did not want to lose the kite.

Although I knew the string was essential to the kite's survival, it seemed the kite was begging to be released from what it perceived as unnecessary bondage. It was as though the kite wanted to cut its only connection to the ground. The irony is amazing. As soon as the kite gets its way, is freed from the string, it is doomed to crash, usually broken beyond repair.

Who Wants to be a Kite?

God-breathed friendships are like boys flying a kite. Sometimes you are the kite and sometimes you are the guy on the ground holding the string.

I am free to be Spirit-blown into whatever God is calling me to be. I am free to catch the highest wind and go to places in the Spirit that I have never explored. But this is because I am in relationship with one or two who I know have my best interest at heart. Their only desire is for my well-being. I am convinced they have no personal agenda, no secret desires or need to profit from any success I may have. I never have to be concerned that they will become jealous or envious of how I am used of the Lord. I am at peace with the knowledge that their prayer for me is pure and their desire for my success is genuine. The counsel I get is intended to bless and encourage, not to dominate or control. Their motivation is not jealousy or envy. It is love. As in any true covenant relationship, their hands are open, willing either to release or be wrong. Their love, prayers, and support do not waver by my decisions.

Conversely, they carry in their heart the same understanding and confidence about my intentions toward them.

This kind of relationship cannot be legislated or assigned. It cannot be determined by geographic region or personality test. It is determined by a heart-to-heart covenant that is tested and proven in the crucible of trial and fire. It develops over time as men and women make a daily conscious decision to respond to others as they themselves want to be loved and cared for. This place of trust in the heart of another can never be imposed; it can only be earned.

To these folks, prayer is more than laying on of hands. To them, genuine relationship is in the laying on of the heart.

The balance is in the Body. Not in me.

The relationship that allows you to be everything you can be is born out of mutual respect, mutual honor, and of course genuine love. These individuals believe in the calling that is on one another's life. They love, pray, trust, and give room to fly even when the skies are not so clear.

The balance is in the Body. It is not in me.

Out of String

Yes, there are times when the person on the ground is out of string. He feels the pressure of the kite pulling on his better judgment as it flies into uncharted skies. Sometimes it takes all his strength and faith to hold onto that relationship. Sometimes he will run down the street so the kite has more room to fly. When he runs out of street, he runs across the field, holding onto that kite string and praying that soon the kite will catch a smooth wind and settle in. Sometimes the way comes to an end and the strength of the string is tested to an extreme measure.

But this situation is exactly why they have been forging a strong bond of covenant all this time. The relationship can stand the test of love and commitment when the mutual sense of covenant has been seared into their hearts.

A broken string benefits no one. Without its tension, the kite falls to the ground. The very thing it wanted and desired becomes its downfall, its destruction. Instead of soaring higher and higher, it finds itself broken on the ground or torn by the limbs of a tree. The thing that gave it the power to soar is the one and same relationship that ultimately keeps it in touch with time and space.

But the kite is not the only one affected. The one on the ground never would have looked up had the kite not been flying. He never would have been challenged to peer into things he has never before seen. If he were not looking up to the kite he would never see the world as his friend sees it. He would have missed an essential element of God's heart for the nations. Because he is holding the kite, he cannot help but be affected by the wind that carries the kite heavenward.

We All Need Someone

Of course, this example will work in nearly every relationship in which we find ourselves engaged. I need the ones God puts in my life, and they need me. The prophetic slobbering of a prophet alone will drown the hearer in mystical saliva. The dusty words of a didactic teacher will choke even the most fervent believer. But when the prophet's slobber is mixed with the teacher's dusty words, they form a salve that will always open the eyes of the blind.

We must let the ones we love fly. For we will never be satisfied until we ourselves are freed to fly.

So we bathe one another in prayer with full confidence in the One who sends the wind and blows it under our wings. This is the freedom to soar.

The balance is in the Body.

Not in me.

Chapter 13 Scripture References

Hebrews 12:11 NAS

II Corinthians 5:17 PEB

Matthew 9:17 PEB

Ephesians 4:11 PEB

Luke 1:37 PEB

Matthew 22:39 PEB

James 1:3 NAS

Romans 8:19 NKJV

Psalms 140:13 NKJV

Colossians 1:5 PEB

Ephesians 4:12 PEB

Isaiah 40:31 NKJV

III John 2 NKJV

God may know everything, but I sure don't. For me, every day is an adventure waiting to happen.

*I humbly
take my place
in the multi-
faceted edge
of God's
plan for
this
planet.*

CHAPTER 14

The Secret of the Serrated Edge

Our heart's desire is to be in the center of all that God is doing. Most of us would do anything for that possibility. Our fulfillment in life is in knowing that we allow Him full sway in our lives. Our heart burns within us at the thought that we are experiencing an interactive fellowship with the living God, who has put us exactly where He wants us, doing precisely what is on His heart for us to be doing.

Surely this is a noble goal.

Would to God that more of His people would be so inclined to seek Him.

But in our search for spiritual relevancy, we have allowed ourselves to define the cutting edge of God's purposes according to the work to which He has called us as individuals or organizations. We have considered ourselves the plumb line of His plan for the nations, being certain there is nothing more anointed to do than the work He has given us. In the course of all that we have touched and prayed for, we are convinced we have become the cutting edge and we alone carry the real purposes of God in our hearts.

Where is the believer who is willing to see the Lord's plan from a perspective other than his own? Who of us is secure enough in Christ alone to share his "powerful revelatory platform" with someone whose calling is different, but just as important as his own?

Who is there among us in whom brokenness has done its work to the point that he has nothing to defend, nothing to prove, and no one to beat?

Where is the one who rejoices when another prospers, gets more recognition, or is promoted to a higher place of influence? Who is content to wait for the loving hand of the Father, who alone promotes, recognizes, and grants authority?

> *Where is the one who rejoices when another prospers, gets more recognition, or is promoted to a higher place of influence?*

But this is the heart of our Lord Jesus. The Church He is building excels in servanthood and humility, building no sweaty, earthly kingdom. The heart of our Lord Jesus is on His Kingdom alone. Those who hear His voice and allow Him to live His dynamic and love-giving life through them will build no other kingdom. Their very life is to do the will of the Lord.

Folks who live in this place will rejoice as God uses people other than themselves. These folks fervently and genuinely pray for those whose passion is different from their own. They see God much bigger than what He has given one person or group to accomplish. They see a God who is not interested in competition or comparisons among His own. They walk softly before Him because He is the plumb line to which the Body of Christ must compare themselves.

Falling into the "Me" Trap

The clamor of carnal jealousies only pollutes the spiritual atmosphere with unregenerate rhetoric that pours from the heart of the envious. That jealousy confuses the soul and reduces the purity of His call to petty issues that arouse fleshy emotions and reveal unsanctified ambitions.

Because we really do not understand the power of Him who dwells within, or the incredible privilege we have as partakers of His abiding Presence, we are all too quick to judge and condemn one another when we do not flow in the same "cutting edge calling."

It is no wonder there is such a flood of E-mails, newsletters, books, and TV shows, all telling us quite clearly (and quite emphatically) that what God has given to them is certainly the closest to His heart and purposes for this generation. Others, with a "lesser" calling, are led to feel inferior to the main issue on God's heart. The main issue, of course, is the issue they carry in their own personal kingdoms.

The Anointing to Do His Will

But ministry does carry with it incredible power. That is why so much is able to be done. Only His power can do the impossible. When we are called to do the impossible, great power is needed. Extraordinary things are done in the earth because of the Presence that is at work from within. In fact, it takes such an incredible supernatural force to do His will that everything else pales in significance to that call. That is as it should be. A call needs intensity of focus, zeal, understanding, and compassion, as well as passion to do what He has given us to do.

The trap, however, is the same one we all fall into—no matter what He has called us to do. Our "focused vision" turns quickly to "tunnel vision" and skews our perspective, giving us an unbalanced sense of importance in relationship to the rest of the Body. All of a sudden, "our" ministry is the most significant one on God's heart. Personal opinion becomes the word of the Lord. We begin to believe that we alone are on the cutting edge.

Remember, great intensity of God's power and grace is essential or we could not do the wonderful things we are called to do, no matter how humble or extravagant those things may seem to be. But we must also remember that it takes this power and grace to do anything of significance in the Kingdom. In the broader, more accurate analysis, no ministry is more important than another. God sees us as peers. But when our view of ourselves becomes tunnel vision, we see ourselves a measure above those whose call is different from ours.

The Great Equalizer

You may be called to open a daycare center, start a prison ministry, or launch a business. You may be an evangelist, prophet, pastor, teacher, or apostle. You may be a teacher or a politician. You may be called to stay at home and raise your children. You may be a reporter or a clerk at a local bank. You may even be called to publish books. Are you doing what God is telling you to do? The power and grace needed to do anything God has told you to do is the same. His mercy and His grace is always the great equalizer among us. When we see all the activities among those who belong to Him, we see the multifaceted desire of our Lord to bring wholeness to all of humanity. This puts our work into perspective. We find ourselves as peers with all those who have said "yes" to Him.

I love to see the Lord do His work in the many-membered Body. Is it tough on the ego? Sure. But it is necessary for me so that I remember I am only part of something much bigger and much more powerful than I can ever be on my own.

I have failed enough to know this in my heart of hearts.

I have commanded my heart in ways that have resulted in brokeness and sorrow beyond any desire to discuss it.

A Serrated Edge

If we were all willing to take a step back and look at the whole Body of Christ instead of only the part God has given to us (important as that might be), we would see that the so-called cutting edge of God's purposes is more like a serrated edge. God is doing many things today that are apparently unrelated and yet vitally interlocked in the heart of the Father. One cannot exist without the other, for in the economy of God our lives are interwoven in supernatural ways that we cannot even begin to perceive.

What part is more essential to our bodies? Let me put it another way. Which is the more "cutting edge" activity in the body? Are lungs more important than hearts? Are blood vessels more critical than the blood they carry? Do these parts argue over which is more important or necessary? Are they not all "cutting edge"? In light of the essential functions needed to keep the body alive and well, are they not all equally critical?

Of course, "cutting edge" sounds much more impressive. It makes me sound like I am ahead of the rest. When I am on the cutting edge everyone must follow me. Everyone looks to me. I am the authority. I am the one who has that special connection with God.

The "serrated edge" is boring. There, I am not the only expert anymore. I must share the platform. No one is looking at me in awe and wonder. On the serrated edge, many, many folks are hearing significant things from the Lord. I must be content as He raises up other faces in the Church He is building. The Church has many faces, all important and all lovely. They all have names. They all have a specific calling. He loves them individually and His plan for them is uniquely theirs.

A nameless, faceless Church is far more exciting—after all I have a name and everyone knows my face.

But for the egomaniac in me, the cutting edge is definitely better than the serrated edge. A nameless, faceless Church is far more exciting—after all I have a name and everyone knows my face.

A Day in the Body

Recently, I got an E-mail from a pro-life group that told me unless I was out blocking abortion clinics with my body chained to a parking meter, I was not in the will of God. A few minutes later I got another E-mail from a national intercessory prayer group that told me if I did not fast and pray for three days before the election, I would be responsible for whatever happened on election day. So I had an anvil of guilt for each shoulder.

Later that day I innocently began opening my mail. The next half hour was an experience that still gives me an occasional shudder. In just thirty minutes I discovered that God only meets in homes; He primarily moves in the arts and pageantry ministry; my financial future hinged on my willingness to buy into a program that was the cutting edge of God's plan for my financial freedom; since my body was the temple of the Holy Spirit, I had to take certain vitamins or I was sinning against my temple; the future of the Church is in celebrating the Jewish feasts and I had to go to a Midwest city to get a cutting edge word from the Lord.

After much prayer, I realized that my only hope of being in God's perfect will was to go to Missouri, form a Messianic congregation that met in homes, put all my money in certain investment funds, worship in angel costumes while blocking abortion clinics and passing out Vitamin C to the passers-by.

Now, before you think I oppose any of these areas I have used as an example, let me quickly say all these areas have their place in God's purposes and are all part of His serrated edge movement in the Body of Christ as a whole. Each has its importance in the many-faceted plan of God in these awesome days. But let's face it. One is not more important than the other in the overall picture of the Body.

Functioning as a Body

I am grateful that my heart concentrates on doing its job precisely seventy-two times every minute. My heart does not have time to exalt itself over my lungs as a more important organ. Personally, I want my heart to mind its own business, concentrating fully on its own ministry and leaving the lungs to my head, which is perfectly capable of directing their activities. After all, my body parts are not in competition; they are co-laborers. Their individual functions are different, but they are intricately and inseparably woven together in purpose and destiny. Their functional unity brings about wholeness and an accomplishment exponentially greater than their individual responsibility, no matter how important we seem to think each is.

Unless the parts are joined, a heart pumps blood onto the ground, accomplishing nothing and ultimately destroying itself for lack of the nourishment it must rely on other body parts to supply in order to survive.

Content and Thankful

Instead of clamoring for the most prominent seats at a banquet, let us rather devote ourselves to the place that God has given us. Let's bless one another in the diversity of His Body. With genuine hearts, not from hidden agendas or unspoken criticism, let's pray for one another. Let's rejoice, from a sincere hope for success, when someone else prospers even beyond our prosperity.

Instead of trying to win over the masses to our cause, we should prayerfully consider how to enlarge what God has done for us, not at each other's expense, but for each other's benefit. All the while we must remember that our call is a part of the mighty handiwork of God among His people.

Just say "Yes."

Our responsibility is quite simple. We simply need to say "yes" to the Lord and all He is calling us to do.

To be sure, God will lead some to join various causes, but we must avoid the guilt of a handful of newsletters that come our way, telling of the wonders and power of the "cutting edge," as though the only way to be a part of the cutting edge is to work for their cause.

God's edge is multifaceted. If you are responding to the Lord, you are where He wants you to be. You are on His serrated edge. You can be a journalist or a stay-at-home mom. You may be a teacher or a store clerk. You may be a missionary or a factory worker. You can be president or a Bible study teacher. The cutting edge for you is when you do exactly what God is telling you to do. Anything else is a cheap imitation and nothing more than wood, hay, and stubble.

If you are doing what God has told you to do, no matter how grand or humble, do it with every ounce of strength you have. Then you can be sure you are part of God's mighty serrated edge.

The world will never see the Lord Jesus high and lifted up until He is lifted up among us, by us and through us—a Body that stands tall, lifting the Head, who is Christ, above all, to be seen by all and worshiped by all.

It is then that the kingdoms of this world will become the Kingdom of the Lord and of His Christ, and He will reign forever and ever.

What is the secret? We are members of one another. Within the veil of His Manifest Presence, He is forever the center of all we do. He is all we please. He is all we need.

Chapter 14 Scripture References

Romans 12:2 PEB
II Corinthians 1:24 NKJV
Galatians 4:7 PEB
Matthew 16:19 NKJV
Colossians 1:18 PEB
Romans 12:1 NKJV

Colossians 3:1 PEB
I John 2:17 PEB
Matthew 17:20 PEB
Matthew 16:18 NKJV
Romans 12:4 PEB

If you are doing what God has told you to do, no matter how grand or humble, do it with every ounce of strength you have.

I repent.
I put myself
and my soul
in Your
all-powerful,
all-merciful
hands.

CHAPTER 15

The Secret of the Judgment

"In Jesus' Name!" the preacher thundered in a powerful surge of faith. His hand lay heavily on the brow of a weeping and hopeful saint. "In Jesus' Name!" His voice again thundered throughout the packed auditorium. Hundreds watched as the man of God concentrated his prayers on the needs before him. A whimpering voice was barely audible over the loudspeakers. "Nothing happened. Nothing happened. I did everything you told me to do, but nothing happened."

Tears streamed down the young man's face as a sense of utter hopelessness filled his heart. He looked up at the man of God in anticipation of help and guidance.

"Do you believe the Word of God?" came the challenging voice of the preacher.

"Yes, yes, I do, but nothing is happening and...and I really don't think anything is going to happen," the young man confessed sheepishly.

"What did God say?" came the nearly mocking reply from the man of God.

"I...I know what God said, er, I know what you said, and I don't know if it was really God or—"

"Thank You, Jesus! Thank You, Lord! You have revealed a spirit of unbelief. How can You move when there is unbelief?"

The preacher turned a pitiful gaze on the young man, having given up on this one ever receiving anything from the Lord. "Go your way, and when you are ready to believe God, come back."

The onlookers gasped with unbelief as a hush swept the auditorium. The man of faith and power turned away with a clear sense of disgust. His face was red with anger and embarrassment. Sweat poured from his forehead as he walked quickly from the platform, leaving behind dozens of people still waiting for prayer. The young man also was left behind with his small family. They lowered their heads in shame and slowly walked back to their seats. His face too was red with anger and embarrassment. Sweat poured from his forehead as he walked, mumbling with merciless personal chastisement.

The young father quietly yet angrily rebuked himself for allowing such a spirit to overcome him. He knew better than that, yet he allowed himself to falter.

His wife looked at him with disappointment and pity. She loved him so much, but how would they ever be used of God with such meager faith and barren knowledge of the Word? The preacher was right. They were trapped in unbelief, and a just God would never bless such weakness. The young mother gathered her children and hugged them tight as she thought of their future with doubt and fear.

The preacher nearly ran to his study. He tossed his Bible onto the couch and threw his arms in the air in total frustration as he paced around the room.

"I can't believe it," he said angrily to the associates who followed him from the podium. "I have never been so embarrassed! So humiliated! No wonder God's judgment is coming to this country!" Sweat stilled poured from his face as he paced the room in utter rage. "No wonder He is through with us. I'm telling you, God's judgment is coming. He is through with our unbelief. He is through with our excuses. He's going to judge us—and the sooner the better!"

The room had grown silent. One man seemed to shudder as he pondered the Judgment. He tried to speak but then thought better of it. This was no time for discussion. Maybe another time, another place, but certainly not here and absolutely not now.

The preacher pointed his finger at his colleagues, shaking it with firm resolve. "From now on," he said with dogged determination, "I'm going to pray for God's judgment on this country. No more mercy! No more chances. In fact, I can feel it in my innermost being. God is going to judge this nation! He is through with it. The Judgment is coming! We had our chance and it's all over. We have had over two hundred years and we blew it. Our time is up. The Judgment is coming, and I can't wait to see it happen!"

With a sense of deserved retribution in his heart, the powerful man of God grabbed his coat and walked out.

The fire certainly followed this preacher over the next several months as he proclaimed his new revelation from coast to coast. The airways reverberated with a message of finality and impending doom. "There is no hope. God is absolutely finished with this country," he said with eloquent anger as he recounted the endless failures of the people of God over the past two centuries, not to mention the Church's utter refusal to hear what God was trying to say through him, an anointed and faithful man of God. God's patience was exhausted. So when the nation finally refused His word, judgment was His only recourse.

From city to city and state to state the prophet carried his urgent and deadly message from a God who was tired of His creation. Other men soon joined in the proclamation, for many shared this man's frustration with the Church and the nation as a whole.

They say adversity makes strange bedfellows. Well, so do frustration and personal offense. Preachers from every denomination and doctrinal persuasion seemed to stampede to join the chorus of voices proclaiming the Judgment. Men who would never have been seen together in fellowship now shared platforms in a unified declaration of what awaited the land. There was no evidence of disunity here, only a continuous litany of fear and doom. God was through with sin, weakness and faithlessness.

It was a strange collection of spiritual misfits, actually. Each one carried his own baggage of spiritual and eternal truths. Some were certain which version of the Bible was correct. Some had cornered the revelation on the Book of Revelation. Others knew better how to take communion, some spoke in tongues, and some most definitely did not. Some believed in a pre-tribulation rapture, some a post-tribulation rapture. Others didn't believe in the rapture at all. Still others didn't believe in the tribulation. Some believed only in home fellowships, some only in corporate gatherings. Others did not believe in gathering at all.

Issues of grand importance were laid aside: how to dress; how to baptize; whose name to pray in; whose church to pray in; how much makeup to wear; who we should associate with, and who we should not associate with; kingdom now or kingdom then or no kingdom at all; Christians in politics; and on and on and on.

How tiresome it all seemed. Yet I guess the vital importance of these issues to His appearing had to be evident to somebody. At least, somebody much more spiritual than I.

Strange bedfellows, indeed. For each man's ambition was usually theologies apart from the ambitions of those who were now joining forces and resources. The only common thread was the Judgment. None of their particular points of view were received and embraced on a grand scale, so their hearts burned in unison with the desire for the Judgment.

It was ironic, really. They all wanted the Judgment, but each for a different reason. In fact, deep in the heart of many lingered the belief that some with whom they now shared the platform would also be on the receiving end of the very Judgment they were jointly proclaiming.

It was quite sacrificial of them, when you think about. And quite courageous. They were willing to share a platform with others who would be judged, risking their own well-being for the sake of the larger Body of Christ.

But all that is not for us to consider just now. After all, the most important thing was what unified them: the Judgment.

Everyone benefited. They all knew just how to seize the opportunity. And seize it they did!

Books were published. Videos were produced. Christian talk shows were soon buzzing with the sense of the impending catastrophe. What would God do? How would He judge us? What could we expect? Experts were called in and very important-sounding analysts analyzed the situation. Everyone had an opinion; some even had determined the dates of the Judgment.

The response of the average believer was quite predictable. The populace was utterly devastated. And why not? They were being told that God had given up on them. Quite a different notion from being under conviction, from which posture one could most definitely repent. But the preacher's point was clear: The Judgment was coming no matter what. There was no more room for repentance and change. God was exasperated with a rebellious humanity and He stood poised to send the Judgment. Prayers were useless now; it was to be every man for himself.

It soon became a dark and frightening time as men frantically charted a course to try to somehow escape the Judgment.

Some were trying to escape to another country with their loved ones. They scurried for passports and combed the globe for a suitable destination to raise a family, earn a living, and, most importantly, escape the Judgment.

But most Christians did not have the financial option simply to "fly away." Their escape would be impossible. They could only try to lessen the impact of the Judgment. Some of these less fortunates attempted to buy land in remote wilderness areas. Some were digging shelters under their homes, and still others installed solar panels or windmills. All of this because of the Judgment. A nation was turning farther from a God who had finally turned on them.

Soon an entire industry emerged as enterprising speculators began to sell everything from dried food to Geiger counters, long-life candles to short-wave radios.

It would truly take a miracle now. Oh, I'm sorry, I forgot—they could not count on that. He had abandoned them.

The Judgment

Our man of the hour returned late one night to his hotel room. It had been a grand meeting. More than a thousand people were now shaking in their boots with terror. But it was good for them. They deserved it. Maybe if they had listened to him a year ago, God would not be planning this. After all, he had spent many years preaching God's love. No one listened. "Well," he thought to himself, "they are listening now. But it's too late. The Judgment is coming and they deserve whatever God decides to do. No amount of praying would be able to deliver them from this one."

With that final thought of personal satisfaction, he crawled into bed and fell into a deep sleep.

He had no idea what was about to happen to him. He had no idea that the events of the next few hours would rattle his personal faith to the very core of his being. He did not realize that the Judgment he proclaimed upon an unsuspecting nation was about to visit him—and it would come with more fury and terror than he could ever have possibly imagined.

I do not think he would have slept so soundly had he realized he was about to be thrust into a depth of horror that would cause him to ask for—no, cry out for—death itself.

The Mission

A loud, relentless knocking at the door reverberated through the silent darkness. The preacher jumped to his feet as though a lightning bolt had struck him. The room was so dark. He ran to the window. Nothing was there but blackness, blackness and silence. The city should have been down there somewhere. But it wasn't. His face pressed against the cold glass as he tried to reorient himself.

The knocking continued shooting adrenaline into his system with each thump. His heart raced in terror. His mind raced for answers.

Why was it so dark?

Where were the lights of the city?

And who the heck was pounding on his door?

He stumbled across the room, kicking the trash can and tripping over his own suitcase.

"I'm coming! I'm coming!" he shouted half in anger and half in confusion.

His head reached the door before the rest of him did. Now he tasted blood in his mouth as he pulled himself up and fumbled for the bolt. Again the knocking. He did not know why he hurried so, nor did he know what awaited him in the hallway. He tried to look through the privacy hole in the door, but he could not seem to focus.

His heart still pounding in fear, he took a deep breath and opened the door to a smiling and somewhat bewildered-looking young man dressed in a red bow tie and jacket. "Evening," the young man said with a reluctant smile. "Room service."

Blood still dripping into his mouth, The preacher staggered to one side as the server wheeled a cart into the room. "Room service?" The server paused to see blood dripping into the preacher's mouth. "Better get used to that taste."

The preacher was exasperated. "Room service? I never ordered room—"

"Oh, yes, you did, my dear sir," the server said as he passed in front of the preacher.

"What are you doing here? I didn't order anything."

The young man ignored him. "Say, haven't I seen you on TV? Aren't you some talk-show host or something?"

The preacher recovered ever so slightly, long enough to explain who he was, the important mission he was on, and why he would have been seen on television.

"I am surprised you have not heard," the preacher said, quite gratified that he was recognized. "God showed me that He was through with this country and all the Christians. I'm telling everyone about the Judgment that is coming because people will not repent. God has uniquely given me this gifting to speak on His behalf." The sinister gleam that came into his eyes every time he talked about the Judgment was hard to miss.

Our oracle from God was so full of himself that he did not notice the server begin to glow with an unearthly light. "God has been giving me opportunities all over the nation to tell people that it is too late. The Judgment is definitely coming, so they need to get ready for it." A sneer of vengeful satisfaction swept his face as he told his story.

Then a deep and thoughtful voice came from out of nowhere. "And what would you, O man of God, decree upon such a nation as this, where sin abounds and hearts are hard?"

Startled by the voice, the preacher turned to find that the server was no longer there. In his place was a man, no, a being of enormous strength and beauty. His voice was full of quiet assurance, and his demeanor was a picture of perfect peace.

"Are...are you from Heaven?" was all our preacher could say. Granted, it was not very creative, but at least he could say something in the presence of an angel.

"I am an emissary from the Lord on high," the angel said. "The Lord Himself has sent me specifically to you for this occasion."

"Are you sure you are here for me? I always thought angels were too busy doing God's will and bringing people to repentance to take time for real men of God," the preacher asked.

"You have no idea," the angel replied, suddenly getting very serious. "Anyway, you are the one with the message, so it is all up to you."

"What's up to me?" the preacher queried.

"Why, the Judgment," the angel said.

"What Judgment?" the preacher asked, a bit startled by his heavenly visitor's message.

The angel was becoming quite impatient. It was going to be a long night, and he was anxious to get started.

"The Judgment! The Judgment! What? Did you forget already? The Judgment. The thing you are talking about every waking hour. The Judgment on the country," the angel responded in utter frustration.

"What do you mean the Judgment is up to me? What do I know about judgment?"

"Apparently quite a bit," the angel responded. "You sure talk about it enough. So the Lord sent me to get your help. I am instructed to tell you that whatever judgment you decree will come upon this nation before the end of the day. It is completely up to you. This country's future is in your hands. You may punish her at your leisure."

The angel pulled the only chair in the room directly in front of the preacher, sat down, and folded his arms.

"Well?" he coaxed.

Our preacher stood rather dumbfounded, so the angel continued to speak.

"Come, come now, don't be bashful. There are plenty of judgments to choose from. How about a good famine? An earthquake? That might leave a lasting impression."

But the preacher didn't hear anything beyond God's offer for him to pick the Judgment. "God wants me to pick the Judgment? God wants *me* to pick the Judgment?" He walked rather aimlessly around the room as he pondered such an important mission. "Ah! God wants *me* to pick the Judgment! He wants me!"

"That's the spirit, my friend, that's, ah-hem, the spirit. Now, what shall it be?" The angel reeled around to confront the preacher face to face. His eyes turned to steel and his jaw locked with gritty resolve. "How shall we bring this nation to her knees in revenge and repentance?"

"Pestilence."

"What?" the angel gasped. The preacher had actually caught him a little off guard.

"You heard what I said. Pestilence. I want to judge the nation with pestilence." The preacher spoke like a man with years of experience.

"You don't know what you are asking," the angel responded. "You have no idea what this will mean."

141

The preacher interrupted him. "I really beg to challenge your concerns. I have been dealing with the likes of these folks all my life, and I tell you that the only thing that will change them is pestilence."

"Then pestilence it will be." The angel's voice roared like the sound of thunder as he threw his arms above him and disappeared in a ball of blinding light.

Out of the darkness and silence that followed loomed an eerie sense that something had just happened in the heavens and was about to visit the earth.

As the preacher stood there, the television came blaring to life. He ran to turn down the volume so he could make sense out of what was happening. A newscaster was crying—yes, crying.

"Scientists are fairly certain they have finally determined exactly what has happened." The newsman tried to continue, but the scenes being broadcast were too terrible for words to describe. The network left him sobbing on a lonely south Florida beach while a stunned anchorman tried to continue from the studio.

"It seems the big storm that blew over Florida last week carried with it an airborne AIDS virus that we suspected existed, but never really saw. The swamps of south Florida apparently acted as an incubator for the virus, which grew faster than anyone thought was possible.

"The virus incubated in the swamp and mutated into a form that seemed to render it fatal with only one incidental contact with the lungs. Death is reported to appear almost painless and is nearly instantaneous."

Nevertheless, death is death, no matter how painless or instant.

"Yesterday's storm blew the virus north and west in the typical counterclockwise movement of air in a low-pressure system. Nearly half the population of Florida has succumbed to the virus. Scientists estimate that 98 percent of the population of Florida will be dead by nightfall."

The preacher stood in silence as the reports continued to come in. He hardly twinged at the pictures from the Orlando area, where an estimated 40,000 men, women, and mostly children died in less than one hour.

Army blockades tried to keep the people from fleeing northward, away from the death virus that crept steadily and relentlessly over the land. But even the military fled at this invisible and most deadly foe.

It almost didn't seem to bother him as the weather satellite tracked the path of the storm carrying its deadly judgment deep into the heart of America. "They deserved it!" He scowled as he turned off the TV, only to have it turn on again of its own accord.

He watched reluctantly as the television, with an apparent mind of its own, moved from channel to channel. Scenes of horror and suffering appeared on each station.

A stadium full of sports fans lay forever silent in Atlanta.

A shopping mall in Memphis became an unwilling sepulcher for hundreds of afternoon shoppers.

The burning wreckage of countless planes at every major airport on the southeastern coast was bleakly displayed. Hundreds of other planes frantically searched for a safe place to land, free from the virus, free from the Judgment.

Highways were littered with twisted wreckage as black and angry smoke rolled furiously skyward, marking each spot of yet more victims of the Judgment.

The television continued its slow, almost monotonous scroll of stations. Some were off the air; some were running old movies as though oblivious to what was happening outside. One station was apparently abandoned, except for two anchormen slumped over their desks, victims of the Judgment. A lone TV camera stood skewed to one side with no operator.

In a surge of triumphant self-righteousness, the preacher once again turned off the TV. "It has begun." He thought to himself. "Finally, I will be vindicated. Finally everyone will see that I was right..."

But his thoughts were interrupted by the television, which once again came on of its own accord. He angrily grabbed the cord, ripped it from the wall, and yanked the other end of the cord from the back of the set, but it again came blaring to life.

"It's as though it's Judgment Day," a nameless voice said with chilling finality.

"Government officials continue to tell us that the plague is contained, but these pictures from around the country tell a much different story. These images are live from Washington, DC" The pictures moved from city to city as the announcer detailed The Judgment like a sportscaster announces the evening basketball scores. "Philadelphia, Newark, Providence, Hartford, Boston, Bangor..." The shroud of death rolled without mercy up the Eastern seaboard, killing everything in its path.

"California always gets off easy!" the preacher shouted with helpless frustration. "I just can't understand it! If anyone deserves the Judgment, Californians do." He pounded the top of the television with both fists in anger.

Suddenly the screen went blank, only to reappear moments later with the sound of his own voice gleefully pronouncing the Judgment. "If anyone sees this man, please call your local police. He is wanted for questioning concerning the virus. Some FBI agents have confirmed that a new hypothesis is emerging surrounding the plague. Health officials are now saying there is absolutely no way this virus could have established this deadly course on its own. They are speculating that it is a possible act of terrorism by a fringe religious group based somewhere on the East Coast."

The TV suddenly scrolled to another station. "What was that?" The man of God suddenly felt cold and clammy. His breathing was becoming more rushed. Suddenly he felt very alone. "Could they really think I might have had something to do with this?" he thought to himself. But he brushed it off with a nervous laugh that didn't really give him any peace.

But the TV blared on from yet another terror-stricken city. Another newscaster continued the almost monotonous review of the macabre terror that gripped the nation.

"Meanwhile, airport quarantine efforts seem to have failed. All planes and passengers from the East Coast are being held in hangars for fear of the Judgment. Hundreds have already died there."

The TV switched to another station. "Here in LA, government officials now speculate that a radical fringe religious element has indeed orchestrated this virus release from the Caribbean."

The preacher pounded the television. "What!" he shouted.

Another announcer continued, "Reports coming in from all over the city indicate that this airborne virus was indeed carried to the West Coast and released into the air. Health officials are convinced it is part of a conspiracy devised by a small religious organization whose intentions are not yet known. Officials say they are searching for the leader for questioning. If anyone sees this man"—the preacher was appalled to see his own picture flashed on nationwide television—"please contact local officials. You should consider him emotionally unstable and very dangerous."

Unparalleled fear now gripped the preacher. With a quick move of desperation, he lifted the TV from its stand and threw it out the window, shattering the glass.

He watched it hit the ground and explode with an unearthly explosion that rose back up to the window and threw him against the wall.

Suddenly the angel appeared before him. The preacher saw the angel's look of deep regret and pity as he lay there.

"What are you looking at me for?" the oracle of God asked the angel indignantly. "They got it all wrong. Angel, you know that! I am not the enemy! I am on God's side, remember? I am the one pronouncing the Judgment."

The angel stood in silence. Our preacher just did not get it. I guess the angel knew that if he gave the preacher enough rope, he just might...well, let's just say it's best not to engage your mouth when your heart is not connected to your brain.

"Tell them, angel. Change things for me! You know the truth!"

The angel finally spoke. "You are not going to make this easy, are you? Just remember, it did not have to be so hard."

"Just what does that mean?" the preacher snapped.

But the angel was through speaking. He was not one to argue. Besides, the next event would speak quite plainly to our righteous man of God. With one final look of pity, the angel clapped his hands and disappeared in a flash of blinding light.

"I wonder what that was all about," the preacher huffed as he crawled into bed. "At least that's all over." The angel was right. The preacher had no idea.

The Second Round

To the preacher, it seemed he had barely closed his eyes when he was rocked by an explosion that threw him far from the comfort of his hotel room, right into the center of the Judgment he himself had contrived and orchestrated. There would be no one to blame for this one. He had told the angel he knew better. He was sure that the Judgment was the only way. Now he would experience it firsthand.

The stench of burning sulfur filled his nostrils and scorched his already parched throat. He had to cough, but he could not. He tried to call out (as if someone were out there to help him), but he could not. He lay face down in melting pavement. His cheeks fusing with the macadam as it bubbled beneath him, the preacher forced his hand into the boiling tar and pushed himself up so he could roll to the side of the road.

His clothes ripped from his body as they ignited in the fiery wind. He rolled over and over until he reached the relative safety of the roadside, rubbing himself in the dirt in a frenzied attempt to put out the fire that covered his body.

He was so riddled with pain that he was not sure he felt anything at all. His hands, now caked with road tar, resembled black bricks.

The fireball was too far away for instant death but too close for him to be spared the torment of the Judgment. Nevertheless, fiery confusion engulfed him from every direction. Blackened ruins crumbled as the earth quaked beneath him. The wind raced across the land, as though itself trying to escape the wicked grip of the Judgment.

The troubled earth grew silent beneath him. But it was a bitter mockery, sending a false sense of hope and relief racing through his pounding heart. It was definitely not over. In fact, it had scarcely begun! It was only the beginning of sorrows, and I am afraid that our preacher would have been quite content had a large building fallen on him right then. Alas, not a single large building was left standing to fall. The land was raped—a flourishing garden turned into a wilderness, unable to refresh, heal, or grow again. It was as though, with one final desperate heave, the earth fell silent into eternal death.

He was utterly alone. No assistants followed closely behind him. No one was there to pray for him. There was no one who even knew his name, had he been recognizable at all.

In absolute desperation, he forced in an excruciating breath of air.

Judged

"In the Name of Jesus!" he bellowed as loud and hard as he could. Unimaginable pain ripped through him. His head whirled and pounded with every word. But all was silent.

"In the Name of Jesus!" he cried again. Nothing seemed to happen. Absolutely nothing.

He was so parched that his cries could not convince even one tear to fall down his blistering and bleeding face.

"In the Name of Jesus!" he cried out one more time before dropping his face into the punishing grit of that nameless roadside. He forced himself to breathe, but his lungs resisted the fumes and odors that filled them. Each breath was a concentrated and excruciating effort to gasp enough oxygen to stay alive. With each breath came a moment of consciousness. But even consciousness mocked him, for it brought with it confusion and a riveting sense of divine betrayal. He soon lay silent, having given in to the reality that he would probably die. So he simply waited on that nameless roadside for death to have its final laugh. He lay there with a thousand thoughts, alone, abandoned, and most assuredly judged.

Blood poured from his face and dripped into his mouth. Somehow he suddenly remembered the words the angel had spoken to what seemed like an eternity ago. Yes, now he was used to the taste of blood, his own blood. The Judgment had done it. The Judgment had defeated him.

For some hideous reason, however, death did not come. He lay there for what seemed like hours. Night had fallen, and the only assurance he had that he was still alive was the horrible stench in his nostrils—and the pain.

The numbing pain seemed to be inside and outside. Every nerve in his body demanded attention as it clamored to deliver protests and pain reports from his dying body. His stomach wrenched in piercing agony and his head throbbed. Pain was everywhere, including a pain lodged deep in his heart.

He rolled over and over as he cried out in agonizing pain. Finally he came to rest on his back and was shocked to hear the sound of someone talking.

"Room service! Oh, excuse me, sir, but did you order room service?" Was he dreaming? Was he dead? Was he hallucinating?

"Oh, never mind, it must be the next body down the road a little," the angel said as he walked away. The preacher could only groan. He forced his now cold, misshapen hand out just in time to brush the angel's leg.

The angel stopped abruptly and turned to the man of faith and power. He stood there a moment, wondering why a man would not allow his heart to melt before God. He knew he could never understand the awesome mysteries of salvation, but it still saddened him that humanity was so stubborn and arrogant.

The rain does certainly fall upon the just and the unjust, does it not?

"It is a fearful thing to fall into the hands of an angry God," the angel thought to himself. "I don't know much, but I do know that it does not have to be this way."

The angel finally broke the silence. "Well, so you are alive. I wonder how that happened? Everyone within a sixty-mile radius of the explosion was slated to die. The Judgment, you know. The rain does certainly fall upon the just and the unjust, does it not? But we do have our quotas before it can officially be called the Judgment."

The angel scanned the landscape, reviewing the countless bodies thrown like rag dolls over the land.

"Yes. Well, it's these humans, you know. They keep mixing up their own natural feelings with the compassion of God. Something doesn't go their way, and all they want is vengeance. 'Call down fire from heaven,' they say. 'Send the Judgment,' they say. If they only knew what their lack of God's wisdom and rampant human fleshy emotions can cause."

The angel stopped only momentarily, nudging the preacher ever so slightly with his foot. The preacher jerked like a man hit by a lightning bolt and then groaned with pain.

"Yes, well," the angel began again, "are you going to stay alive long enough for the next event? It gets much more exciting from here."

The preacher tried to speak, but his parched throat prevented him.

"What did you say?" The angel bent over to try to hear him.

"Oh, I'm sorry, you must be desperately thirsty." The angel pulled a long-stemmed glass of ice water from a tray. The soothing moisture relieved the man's thirst and restored his damaged voice box enough to talk.

"The next event? You mean there is more? When is this all going to end?" he whispered as best he could.

"Well, sir, you have no idea how large the mercy of God is. If His mercy prevails, I am sure it will last as long as it has to. God's mercy always has your best interest at heart," the angel replied.

"What are you talking about?" The preacher tried to sound confused, but it was a meager attempt, for they both knew better. The angel did not respond. It was certain that the only way this would truly understand mercy would be to experience for himself. But he was not through with suffering quite yet.

"Please tell me I am dreaming," the preacher whispered. "Please tell me I am still in the hotel room and that this is just a very bad dream."

The angel had an uncanny ability to ignore any question he deemed too ridiculous to answer. This was one of those moments when the whining questions would not be answered.

You delighted in describing a God whose grace was limited and whose mercy was reserved for a select few who were just like you.

"Does it hurt?" the angel asked with no pity and only a little sarcasm. "I thought you wanted the Judgment. I thought you were praying for it. Your mouth watered and your heart raced every time you talked about it. You had a gleam of utter satisfaction every time you walked off the platform, leaving the people with no hope and no answers. You loved painting a picture of God that was vengeful and morbid. You delighted in describing a God whose grace was limited and whose mercy was reserved for a select few who were just like you. Well, it seems to me that you got what you wanted."

The preacher rolled his eyes in pain. "Please. Please tell me this isn't happening."

"Okay," the angel responded rather offhandedly. "It isn't happening."

"Thank God!" was all the preacher could say as he lay back on the ground, positioning himself to be, well, I guess he thought he would be transported back to his hotel.

The angel stood silently for a few minutes as the preacher continued to lie there in pain. Finally he looked up in exasperated impatience.

"Are you there, angel?" he shouted.

"I am standing right here," the angel dutifully responded with an honorable salute.

"Why am I still here? Why am I still lying here in such terrible pain?"

"Well," the angel began, "I suspect it is because less than sixty miles away, one of your nasty human weapons of destruction exploded just a few hours ago, and you happened to be in the neighborhood. Excellent timing, if I do say so myself."

"But you said that it really didn't happen," the preacher protested.

"But that was only because you told me to tell you that."

The preacher lay there in utter disbelief. "You can't be serious! This can't be real! You must make it go away! Take me back to the hotel!" His voice was all but gone again as he sobbed. He tried to wipe his eyes with his hands, only to feel the gritty asphalt melted into them.

"Oh, so now you want it to be a dream? Now you are concerned?" the angel queried. "You were the one preaching the Judgment. You were the one who begged God for this to happen," the angel tormented him.

"I never thought it would come to me! I never thought I would be judged. Surely God will have mercy. Surely there is room in His heart for forgiveness," the preacher said desperately to the angel.

Mercy. Forgiveness. Strange coming from a man like you. Strange indeed.

"Mercy. Forgiveness. Strange coming from a man like you. Strange indeed. It has been a long time since words of that caliber passed through your lips. Mercy? Forgiveness? Don't you remember? Your god removed these words from his active file. They have no meaning now, do they?"

"I just do not understand," the preacher whined one more time. " I just don't see why this is happening to me, of all people! Have mercy on me, O God!"

"You have denied God's mercy to a nation, and now you would ask for it yourself as if you have some special exemption?" the angel said. "Next you will be asking for His grace."

"Yes, oh yes, His grace would be so grand in an hour of torment such as this," the preacher said.

"And precisely where were your prayers for mercy and forgiveness when the Judgment fell on the others?" the angel asked.

"Well, they deserved it."

"And you don't?"

The preacher was silent, stunned by a view of himself he had, up until now, not taken the time to notice. There, in the silent torment of his own judgment, a miracle began to happen. In a very remote part of his heart, far from his own consciousness but close to the Spirit of the Lord, an ever-so-small miracle began to happen. His heart started to soften.

The angel waited. He knew the preacher was close. His response in the next few minutes would determine his fate. Life and death hung in the balance. The Judgment was ready to continue in the preacher's life. The next chapter was waiting to unfold. But the angel raised his hand and held it back. Mercy was triumphant over judgment as the angel waited for a response from the man of God.

He watched closely as a single tear fell from the preacher's eye. As it fell, it washed a streak of soot and sorrow down his face. The man's heart was melting. A little miracle was turning into a major one. The beginnings of a soft heart would soon result in full and utter repentance.

It was time for the angel to speak again. "Tired and frustrated leaders take out their pain on an innocent and trusting following. You were called to shepherd the flock. So they looked to you for hope and encouragement. They needed you to understand their human weaknesses just as Jesus understood the dark night of your soul. You know, those dark and desperate places in your life that you hate and hide because you cannot be free of them.

"Jesus always draws these people in love and forgiveness because He understands their frailty, as you should, since you too are beset with weaknesses and temptations.

"But you didn't care about their pain. You only needed their correct response to further your own agenda. You violated the most sacred trust of the Lord Jesus, who gave you the hearts of His people to nurture and love. The Lord wrestles His people from insecure and angry folks such as yourself. He is building hope into their hearts, not fear and condemnation. God gathers those you are quite willing to scatter and heals those you are content to see die. All because they do not see as you see."

The preacher wept aloud. "No, no, I cannot bear to hear more. I simply cannot bear it!"

The angel fell to his knees in front of the preacher. Grabbing him by the arms, he spoke directly to his heart. "You have no choice in the matter. You have already prayed that everyone would know the sin for which they are judged before they die. You have only a few minutes to live, and my list is still quite lengthy."

The angel cheated a little. He should not have told the preacher he was about to die. (It was the mercy thing again. God's just full of it.) It did, however, help the preacher to focus again.

The preacher managed to pull himself away from the angel's grasp as he cried out to God. "O God, take my life that I might be free from this torment! Why did I have to survive this holocaust? Why did I have to live? Take my life, I beg You. I cannot stand the pain in my body, and the haunting of my soul is far more than I can bear."

The angel stood up in silence. This was always the most exciting part of his missions, for when a man turns to the Lord, his heart is restored and his spirit is healed.

The preacher could not control the thoughts and memories that now passed through his mind. His ruthless treatment of a family in such serious need flashed by. The sorrow and disappointment they suffered pierced his heart like a dagger.

"You are feeling the pain of rejection," the angel told him solemnly. "But not only the pain of this little family. You also are feeling the pain in the heart of the Lord for your rejection of these little ones. You painted a picture of an angry and impatient God just because you were angry and impatient. You are the one who wanted the Judgment. You are the one who wanted those who did not perform for you to suffer. Their picture of the Lord is now skewed, and their disappointment is about to shipwreck God's plan for their lives."

"No! No! They didn't believe God! They didn't believe His Word!" the preacher defended himself. His heart was melting, but a war still raged within him.

"No," the angel responded more gently, "they didn't believe *you*. And they didn't perform for *you*. So you became frightened."

"Preacher," the angel asked him, "have you faced the fears and weaknesses within yourself as these precious ones did in front of you and thousands of others that night?"

With every ounce of strength within him, the preacher forced himself to stand up. The pain throbbed relentlessly through every muscle, and even coursed through his bones.

Tears streamed down his face as he saw The Judgment he had personally pronounced over countless thousands he had been entrusted to care for and pray for. He looked around him and saw thousands of charred and broken bodies over the landscape. He knew it was all because of The Judgment, his judgment.

He saw his own bitterness weaving itself through the insecurity of his own weaknesses, covered with the veil of ruthless religiosity. It tangled its way through every relationship and marred everything he had ever hoped to accomplish. The anger that raged in his heart toward himself he had directed toward the weaknesses of others.

He fell to his knees in shame. He groveled on the ground as though to dig a hole large enough to die in. Tears streamed like rivers as he cried out to God. Repentance was actually beginning.

The angel kneeled with him, wept with him, healed him. The angel knew that God was a loving God. He would forgive this preacher. God would also free His people from the control of other leaders as well; leaders whose hearts were full of the Judgment.

The angel whispered softly, through his own tears, to the weeping preacher. "God builds pathways of love and not walls of doctrine and theology that separate and condemn."

"Forgive me, O God. Forgive me, O God, if You are able. I have sinned to the depths of my very soul. If mercy has come to an end, it is my sin that has exhausted it, not the struggles of Your people. I have mistaken my anger for Your indignation. I have forgotten Your mercy. I have forgotten the pit where You found me and so mercifully dug me from. My pride and my haughtiness deserve nothing less than death. But please, in Your mercy, grant that these, Your own special treasures, which I have abused, not suffer for my sin.

"Grant them healing and restoration according to Your kind intentions and Your tender mercies, which I beg, O God, would be inexhaustible. But as for me, I deserve all that I am suffering, and I leave myself and my soul in Your all-powerful, all-merciful hands."

The preacher fell face down to the ground. He struggled for consciousness, but could keep hold on it no longer.

The wind blew briskly over the sullen landscape. A damp chill swept the early morning as the sun began to rise on the third day of the Judgment. The preacher struggled for life as the angel of death appeared and demanded the first angel to relinquish the preacher's soul. But the server-turned-angel would not release him and, in a final, glorious act of mercy, the angel of death was ordered away in a flurry of thunder and wind. The preacher was left lying alone in the early dawn.

The preacher was suddenly startled by a loud knocking. The sound so frightened him that he fell out of bed.

Reaching the door, he fumbled with the bolt while the knocking continued. He finally swung open the door to a curious-looking young man with a familiar smile.

"Room service!" the young man called. "His mercies are new every morning. It's a new day!"

The preacher leaned against the wall, his pajamas soaked with sweat. Although utterly exhausted, he smiled back at the attendant. "You look silly in that red bow tie."

The angel rolled the table serving cart past the preacher.

"You don't have to dress like that anymore. After last night, I'll know who you are no matter how you dress."

"I know," said the angel, "but it's easier on the rest of the guests. By the way, I took the liberty of calling your secretary this morning. I canceled all your engagements. She said you sounded peaceful, different, somehow."

The preacher didn't look surprised. "Yeah, I don't have the foggiest notion of what to preach now," he confessed.

"Your journey," the angel responded.

"My what?"

"Your journey. Preach your journey." The angel offered again with a smile. "It's the only real thing any human has, preacher or not."

"Oh," the angel continued while he served the preacher breakfast, "I also made an appointment for you to visit a certain family deeply in need of your love and acceptance."

The preacher stood in silence. "I guess I have a lot of talking to do outside the pulpit for a while."

"True repentance always produces change," the angel responded with resolve and finality.

"You are not going to give me an inch on this, are you?" the preacher asked hopefully.

But the angel only smiled and said, "Nope!"

The preacher looked at the angel and suddenly grew quite serious. "If this was all just a vision, then it didn't really happen, did it? I mean, it wasn't really real, was it? Had I not turned, what would have happened? How much of that was real?"

The angel chose his words carefully.

"The pain in your heart and the angel of death would have prevailed had you not responded to the Lord's plea for repentance. His mercy is boundless."

Suddenly a little nervous, the preacher quickly asked, "What does that mean? Do I need to see a doctor? Is my heart failing?"

"No, no, no," the angel smiled. "That's the whole point. Your heart is just fine now."

The angel patted the preacher on the back as he walked toward the door. "Make your repentance complete. Go see these young folks, bare your heart, and let the Word become flesh in your life right now. It will be with you then forever."

The angel continued slowly toward the door. "I'm probably not going to see you again. I am sure there is someone else waiting to experience God's mercy," and he walked out the door.

The angel was wrong. He did see the man of God one more time. In a small house in the suburbs, a few nights later, tears of repentance filled the eyes of the preacher once again.

This time the preacher's head was not in the murky loneliness of a distant darkness, but buried in the shoulder of the young man he had rebuked not long ago.

As husband and wife forgave and prayed, our angel was sent from the throne of God with a pitcher of healing balm, which he generously poured over these loving believers. Christ was formed in their midst that night, and a strength was born that would carry their friendship for a lifetime.

For the secret is simple: The Judgment is not shared. It is God's alone. Human judgment is a disease that runs out of control in the Holy Place where men position themselves for power and favor. In the Most Holy Place, where man sees himself for who he truly is, he throws Himself upon God's mercy. He entrusts his life, his future and his soul to the Lord, in whom he completely rests. Judgment has been removed from his vocabulary and his heart. All that remains is love. The natural flow of this love is toward the rest of humanity in desperate need of God's mercy and grace.

Let God judge.

Let us love.

Chapter 15 Scripture References

Hebrews 4:12 NKJV

Romans 7;13 NKJV

Revelations 14:7 NKJV

Romans 4:10 NKJV

I Corinthians 1:8 NKJV

Psalms 7:11 NKJV

Proverbs 3:5 NKJV

Hebrews 9:27 NKJV

Jude 6 NKJV

Luke 5:32 NKJV

Revelations 11:11 NKJV

Hebrews 3:7 NKJV

Romans 9:15 NKJV

Psalms 136 NKJV

Human judgment is a disease that runs out of control in the Holy Place where men position themselves for power and favor.

*I am
more than
I have
believed. He
loves me
more than
I have
under-
stood.*

The Most Exciting Test You Will Ever Take!

You are about to take a test.

But don't worry. This will be the most exciting test you have taken in a long time.

I guarantee you will love it.

It is not the kind of test you think it is.

It does not measure how badly you have fallen short. It shows you things about yourself that probably no one else has ever shown you. This test will help you to see how far you have come in your heart's desire for the Lord. I know you truly desire Him or you would not be reading this book.

Your heart teaches you a lot about who you are and what you love. I know, we have been told that the heart is deceitful above all things. Under the old covenant that was true. In the New Covenant, God writes His laws gently and lovingly upon our hearts. There is nothing deceitful about that. But as long as we think our heart is deceitful we will follow the rules of the secularized system lords, who know little about a changed heart and nothing about a true personal relationship with Jesus.

Oh, if we would only be free to believe what we truly hear and feel deep inside our hearts!

But, alas! Believing things we have never been taught by man is quite dangerous and near to big trouble—or so they say. I think some have forgotten that the Holy Spirit is the One and true Teacher. He is the One who tenderly and lovingly writes His law on our hearts, in spite of the controlling interests of man. One thing is for certain: When the Holy Spirit teaches us, the truth will never go away. Some will certainly try to steal it away. But what He has taught us will always ring aloud inside. For what the Holy Spirit teaches us is a living testimony of an encounter we have had with the living God that can never be crushed or destroyed.

You Are More Than You Have Become

There is more inside of you than you think. The truth of who you are is more powerful than you have been permitted to believe. But you now have permission to believe the truth that burns within you. Now you have permission to accept what your heart is trying to tell you.

This test will help you to see yourself as you really are. It will help you to see yourself as He sees you, as He loves you, as He embraces you.

I know, I know, we are always judging ourselves by our failures, our pain, and our broken places. But He sees from a totally different perspective.

He sees what He has redeemed.

He sees what He has healed.

He sees what He has dreamed for us.

This test will help you adjust to His way of seeing things, to His way of seeing you.

So here we go. Keep track of your answers!

1. Do you fear the Presence of God, or do you love the Presence of God?

Sounds like a trick question, but it isn't. The question can also be asked another way. "Are you a Levite, or are you from the priesthood of Melchizedek?" Another way to ask this question might be, "Can you minister in His Presence, or must you fall in His Presence?"

When Solomon dedicated the Temple, the Scriptures say that the cloud of glory was so great it spilled out of the Most Holy Place into the Holy Place, where it was technically not supposed to go. The Levites, who ministered in the Holy Place, were accustomed to the Presence behind the veil. They did not know what to do with the Presence when He did not stay where He was supposed to stay. They were therefore overcome with fear. When the Lord was behind the veil, He was contained. The Levites knew what to expect from Him as long as He stayed there. The Levites could get away from Him by staying in the Holy Place, with eleven layers of curtains separating them from their Lord. But when His glory spilled out into the Holy Place, everything was different. None of the rules seemed to apply anymore. Certainly God was not following the rules He Himself had established. His Presence was no longer limited, or shall I say, no longer controlled?

On their Faces

Since the Levites were not accustomed to the Presence of God in their sphere, they fell on their faces with fear, unable to do the work of the priesthood. They loved to do the work of God in their own realm, under the control of the five senses and according to very defined rules of engagement. But this was something else altogether. God was moving out of His own parameters. Unlike Melchezidek, the priesthood of the Presence, the priesthood of the Believer, you and I, the Levites could not become accustomed to sensing His movements and changing their plans as the Lord moved among them.

The Levites were not and are not the priests of the Presence. They didn't know what it was to abide in the Presence of God. Since they did not know Him, they never could have imagined that He wanted only to be close to the ones He loved. This was a most compelling foreshadowing of David's Tabernacle and the tabernacle of the Lord within the hearts of His people under the New Covenant.

Only Melchizedek, the priest of the Presence, you and I, can stand in the Presence and worship in the Presence. Melchizedek represents the only priesthood that can minister in the Presence of God without fear. In fact, this priesthood ministers in His Presence with joy unspeakable! His Presence brings strength and peace. His Presence brings wisdom and sonship. But here is the best news. Melchizedek is the priesthood of the New Covenant. It is for everyone. There is no one turned away! All may freely enter and experience His Manifest Presence moment by moment.

There will emerge a generation of Melchizedek who minister in His manifest Presence. The world, as we know it now, cannot be won with the charismatic parlor tricks by which the faithful are so easily amused. If the world is going to be won, and it will be won, His Presence will manifest Life through a people who can freely walk in His Presence and minister His Presence to a world now in the grip of the enemy.

For years the Lord showed us that He had the power to knock us over; now He wants to show us He has the power to make us stand.

For years the Lord showed us that He had the power to knock us over; now He wants to show us He has the power to make us stand. No more Holy Place antics. I want to stand. I want to stand in wisdom, love, power, and wholeness. I want to stand against the enemy and minister the fullness of Jesus in the presence of any opposition. This does not mean that folks should not be slain in the Spirit. It does mean that we should not be amused by or content with the outward. The individual, the family, the Church, the nation, and the world are only changed when the Kingdom is planted and established within our hearts and minds.

The Levites were priests of the Holy Place. They were never intended to stand in the Presence. In the Holy Place, they tended to the types and shadows of the Ancient of Days but did not actually experience the pulsating power of His manifest Presence as the priests of the Presence did.

Not their Job

Before Christ, the Melchizedek of God, came, the Levites had to do the work of the Most Holy Place, for He had not yet appeared.

The Levites did the work of a priesthood that was not their own. No wonder they were filled with fear when they had to enter the Presence. They feared the Presence, for they were not called or anointed to do the work that is required there.

But Melchizedek loves His manifest Presence. Because Melchizedek was and is the Priest of the Presence, He freely entered the Presence, not out of obligation but out of the sheer joy of experiencing His appearing.

No Fear of Death

The fear of death also haunted the Levites who attempted to enter the Most Holy Place. They did not belong there. They were in a dimension of Spirit for which they were not prepared to live. So death was a real fear for them.

Melchizedek, on the other hand, was not afraid to die because He had already died, and rose from the dead. He belonged in the Presence. He was at home in the Presence. He was and is a friend of the Presence. In fact, Melchizedek, once entering the Presence, never left but took His seat at the right hand of His Father, on the Mercy Seat, where He ever lives to intercede on behalf of you and me, who are also seated there with Him.

I love His Presence. I covet His Presence. I am part of the company of priests that forms a new royal order of believers under the banner of Melchizedek. But this is nothing special, for the Blood washed everyone and prepared each one of us to be seated with Christ within the veil of the Most Holy Place.

If you chose "I love His Presence," you are probably living in the Most Holy Place.

2. Is your goal to act like Jesus, or do you want to yield to Jesus so He can live His life through you?

I cannot think of a more depressing pastime than trying to act like the Son of God.

I compound failure upon failure trying to emulate His love and forgiveness. The longer I live, the more I am convinced that I will utterly fail with each attempt to act like Him, love like Him, be patient like Him, or do anything like Him.

There is no doubt about it, acting like Jesus is a losing proposition.

One morning, during one of my more frustrating times of prayer, I heard the Lord speak softly to my heart.

"What are you doing, Nori? What is your problem? Why are you so weary?"

"Oh, Lord, I'm trying to act like You."

"Oh, you are? How do you think you're doing?"

"Well, sometimes I don't think I'm doing very well. In fact, Lord, most of the time it is quite depressing"

"I don't think you're doing very well either. If the plan of our Father could come to pass by you acting like Me, I would have never had to come. When are you going to give up trying to act like Me and just yield to Me? Why do you try to act like Me when I am living within you and I am perfectly capable of living My life through you? In fact, that is the way it is supposed to be."

"Does this mean I have to take off the bracelet?"

Thank God.

There is a much easier way to let the world see Who is living inside me. I do not have to act like Him anymore than I have to dress a certain way to let the world know that Jesus is alive in me. He actually lives within me! The minute I understand this, I stop trying to look good and be good and do good. Jesus is now free to show Himself to the world through me. The world does not want to see me. I have no wisdom, no healing, no compassion for the nations, but He has all those things and more.

With great joy and a whole lot of relief, I declare to the world and all it contains, "I have been crucified with Christ."

With great joy and anticipation and a whole lot of relief, I declare to the world and all it contains, "I have been crucified with Christ; and it is no longer I who live, but Christ lives in me; and the life which I now live in the flesh I live by faith in the Son of God. For Christ in me is the hope of His glory in the earth."

Christ in me is the hope of His glory shining through me.

If you die to yourself daily and your heart's desire is for our Lord Jesus to manifest Himself to the world through you every day, there is a good chance that you are living within the Most Holy Place.

3. Do you still fight the devil, or is your war over?

Christians love to fight. Seems as though the day has hardly been worth it if we have not had a good bout with satan. It is as though we feel we have really done our part if we engage the enemy.

But our fighting days have mercifully come to an end. The struggle and sweat to protect, cover, explain, and prove are finished.

Our war is over.

We are right with God. There is nothing the enemy can do to keep us from our beloved Lord. The battle for our righteousness ended when Jesus was raised from the dead by the awesome power of His Father. God broke through the gates of hell itself and lifted Jesus to His Father. He was ushered into the Most Holy Place, not by type but in reality, where He will never have to leave His Father's side again. Now He sits on the Mercy Seat, not a shadow, but the real throne of God.

Isaiah saw this happen when he said:

> *"Speak kindly to Jerusalem; and call out to her, that her warfare has ended, that her iniquity has been removed, that she has received of the LORD'S hand Double for all her sins."*

Just think of it! Our sins are forgiven, thrown into the sea of forgetfulness. Our guilt and shame are removed by the Blood of Jesus. Nothing can renew the battle for our righteousness. Jesus already won it for us. Anything we do now to gain God's favor is wasted time and energy. You have His favor.

Your war is over.

Yes, you are human.

Yes, you will fail.

But His love for you is exponentially greater than your sin and failure. Your puny attempts at rebellion cannot remove the love of the Father's heart toward you. Your repeated inability to resist sin is a reminder of your need for Him. Your failures are not spiritual triggers that release condemnation and shipwreck your life.

His Life is Greater than your Failure

You are washed. You are cleansed. The power of His life is far greater than the power of your failure. He wants you to move on. He will deal with the sin and failure. Your repentant attitude and the knowledge of your need of His mercy and love is a constant reminder that you are not an infidel or a failure. Your tearful softness toward Him in times of failure is evidence of a heart that is broken in love to your heavenly Father, who is at work to bring you into your destiny.

The power of His Life is far greater than the power of your failure.

He wants to show you the dream He has for you. He wants you to spend the rest of your life fulfilling the reason you were born rather than trying slavishly to gain the favor of One who already loves you as much as God can love anyone.

I know this will take years of re-programming and re-education unless we have a revelation of His love. For we have been told again and again that His favor is conditional. Salvation is by grace but...but what? We must put our "buts" behind us and accept the fact that our war is over. There is no more struggle for approval. There is no more work to gain favor.

Your unnecessary struggle for approval keeps you weak, tired, and depressed. It keeps your focus on yourself. Your energy and anointing are constantly depleted just trying to gain something you already have: God's approval. For He did not save you to populate heaven. He saved you to be a part of His vast generational army that is establishing His Kingdom on the earth.

The world has yet to see what could happen through a people who know they are forgiven.

Forever Off Balance, Forever Weak.

Much of the time we can see what He has called us to do. We can feel what He has called us to do. In many cases we can even experience what He has called us to do. There are fleeting moments when His grace wells up within and we allow Him to break the power of guilt for a moment of time.

During those rare instances, we feel like we can change the world.

That is because we can.

We feel as though we have the faith of Abraham.

That is because we do.

During those times when guilt and condemnation are overcome, we feel as though we have all the power of God at our fingertips.

That is because we do.

It is as though He could speak through us, love through us, heal through us—do anything He wanted to do through us, and it would work.

And we would be correct.

But it seems as though everything and everyone around us bombards us with accusations that keep us far from His glory and far from the dream He has dreamed for us. We seem to be forever off balance, forever weak.

However, keeping God's people off balance has its advantages. It keeps congregations attending, serving, and, most importantly, giving.

The entrenched system of religion cannot trust the Melchizedek of God with the truth of who the 'common folk' really are and what God has actually done for them. They have no confidence that people who know what Jesus did for them would keep serving the Lord. Further, what would happen if God's people began to hear the Lord for themselves? What would happen to God's people if they knew they were forgiven?

The Reformation occurred when the Bible was made available to the common folk. For the first time, people could read the Word for themselves. It was the end of oppressive, degrading religion for millions who then began to understand and experience God's love for themselves.

The religious system was finally penetrated when men and women began to know God through their own interactive, one-on-one relationship with Jesus Christ.

The wall of control and separation came down.

The cast system began to crumble, and the division between clergy and laity was finally challenged. The words of mere mortal men no longer carried the weight of God's Word. Fear of excommunication, accusations of heresy, torture, and even execution could no longer stop the flow of God's love and power.

God was out of the box of organized and controlling religion.

The same reformation is needed today.

It is much closer than most people think.

Men and women have become weary of the empty words of a lifeless system. These words offer promises that fall to the ground as soon as they flow from the lips of those who are committed to protecting themselves above the dream that God Himself has dreamed for humanity—the dream that began before the foundations of the earth.

The Truth is Getting Out

God's people are forgiven that they may serve the Lord in freedom and fullness of power, love, and compassion. The world is doomed to continue its downward spiral unless someone begins to believe God before they believe a man. True change will never happen as long as genuine believers continue to be intimidated by those with an agenda of self-preservation and personal kingdom building. These will continue to deceive and mislead the true royal priesthood, the priesthood of His Presence, until someone rises up and says, "Stop!"

"Speak kindly to Jerusalem, comfort, comfort My people and declare to her that her warfare is ended."

You who have repented of your sin and your waywardness; you who are trusting Jesus for the times you fail and fall short, your war is over.

Finally.

Completely.

It is time to change the world.

4. Is worship something you do on Sunday, or are you *becoming* worship to the Lord?

Worship is the art of entertaining God through the sacrifice of our body, soul, and spirit to His service and pleasure. It is the moment-by-moment yielding to Him, anticipating the sound of His voice and warmth of His breath. Worship is abandoned confidence that one can trust Him in all things.

Certainly, our worship in songs and hymns and spiritual songs reflects true willful worship, as it should. But when the music stops, the lights of the church are turned off and the front door is locked, true Most Holy Place worshipers continue to worship. For in the dimension of all-God, worship is not an event in time; it is a lifestyle that transcends time and space, consuming body, soul, and spirit. It occurs independently of the circumstances of life and is a continuous event driven by unconscious desire.

It is the incense of love and devotion that rises from the inner being and reaches the Lord as an ever sweet smelling fragrance.

Here, the soul responds to the Presence, who is always nourishing, always healing, always strengthening, always enjoying, and always speaking encouragement to the soul either in word or in spirit.

Worship is a spiritual testimony to every spirit in the heavenly realm that you live for Him. Your spirit is a living, vibrant beacon of blinding light that testifies by your mere existence that the God of Abraham, Isaac, and Jacob is alive and is worshiped among men. It can be recognized in this dimension, and it is a constant distraction to the workers of darkness who would love to hide in the shadows of that dimension. In spite of what any authority, power, or dominion may say, your existence is a reminder of the death sentence wrought upon evil when God raised Jesus from the dead and seated Himself within the veil of humanity itself, forever to rule and reign from His true throne room, your heart.

For our breath is a heavenly opus that permeates every dimension and calls to continuous attention the fact that He who exists outside of time but transcends all dimensions is still supreme in all the universe.

In this dimension every breath, every word, every heartbeat is worship unto the Lord, and everything in the spirit world knows it. Worshipers in this dimension are blinding lights to the darkness and continuous proclamations to the heavenlies that divine love has invaded humankind and has been rooted in the hearts of those who have said "yes" to Him.

In this dimension every breath, every word, every heartbeat is worship unto the Lord, and everything in the spirit world knows it.

"I urge you therefore, brethren, by the mercies of God, to present your bodies a living and holy sacrifice, acceptable to God, which is your spiritual service of worship."

If worship is your lifestyle, you are Melchizedek, indeed, a priest of the Presence, living within the veil of the Most Holy Place.

5. Do you tithe from your increase, giving the Lord His portion, or have you become the tithe, the Lord's portion to the earth?

In the Most Holy Place, the selfish, me-centered spirit of personal desire and ambition beautifully gives way to the glorious freedom of trusting Jesus in everything. Then we can see from His viewpoint, daring courageously to take our eyes off ourselves and our personal needs and wants, that we might see His plan without the tarnish of selfishness. From within the veil, we see the world, or that part of the world He shows to us, from His point of view, the way He sees it, the way He loves it, the way He wants to transform it. We find ourselves yielding to Him, in spite of our own perceived needs and desires, knowing without a doubt that if we would just seek His kingdom, everything that concerns us will be covered. I am my Beloved's and He is mine. He takes care of me.

A Moot Point

It needs to be said. The tithe question under the New Covenant is absolutely moot. But keep reading. What you are about to discover is most exciting.

I am His. He cares for Me as I care for my own children. Bargaining with God or assuming that He will withhold blessing until I "pay up" is anathema to genuine relationship. I am His portion to the nations. I will go where He leads me. I will do what He urges me from within to do.

God really does not need your money.

He needs you.

You are the dwelling place of the Most High. He needs your "yes." He wants your abandoned trust in His love and plan for you. Nothing less than this will give you true peace, and nothing less releases the incredible dream He has dreamed for your life.

We are His Portion

God's intention is that now, in this life, the struggle of control in the Holy Place should give way to the utter peace of releasing personal control to the Lord. My "career" move now becomes the daily routine of releasing the Spirit of God to do what He pleases with me, in me, to me, and through me. I have surrendered control to Him because I have determined that there is nothing more fulfilling than knowing I am in His will. For I am His portion. There is nothing safer than knowing I am being directed by the One who sees the end from the beginning and the beginning from the end. I have relinquished control to the One who has dreamed a dream for me and wants nothing more than to see that dream come to pass sooner rather than later in my life.

Our tithe, represented by 10 percent under the Old Covenant, was merely a prophetic foreshadowing of the right of ownership under the New Covenant. Namely, I am no longer my own.

Jesus did not die for the money in a your wallet. He gave Himself for the one carrying the wallet. He is not interested in arguing about how much money a person should give in the offering. Something far greater than that is at stake here.

I have been purchased by the Lord for His exclusive use. Under the New Covenant, I am no longer under obligation to tithe a minimum amount of money. But that does not relieve me of my responsibility before God. Now He owns me. I do not own myself. The One who owns me and everything I represent now determines my giving. He may ask for anything; I am an eager giver.

> *I have been purchased by the Lord for His exclusive use.*

I do not need to be intimidated into giving. The parlor games of those who try to strip God's people of their hard-earned cash for their own selfish plans do not work. For I do not need to strike a deal with God. I do not need to bargain with Him for a guaranteed return on my giving. Nor do I need to remind Him of what He promised if I give. I know Him and He knows me.

When the Lord wants something from me, He simply asks. I freely give to Him at His inner urging. Gone are the days of being moved by tearful presentations and passionate pleas. I am moved by Him and Him alone.

I am here, like the old prophet, waiting and eager to respond to Him. "Here I am, Lord! Use me! Use me!" Such a relationship is not only possible, it is what He intends for those who call upon the Name of the Lord, our Lord.

I do not tithe in the traditional sense or in any other sense. I have become the tithe of the Lord to the nations. Everything is now a matter of decision by the One who possesses my reins. I am His portion. I have become the portion He has laid aside for Himself to plant His Kingdom in the earth. I am His to be used by Him whenever and wherever He needs me. He now possesses me for a purpose. He will transform and complete all that concerns me.

The Dream is Not for Us

Am I special? No.

Is this dream of the Lord limited to just a few select people on earth? Absolutely not.

But we control the course of our lives until we give that control over to Him. It is simply a matter of concluding that we believe He has a plan for us and that His plan is far better than our plan. The forces of heaven are released on our behalf. As a result, our lives become one miracle after another. These miracles are not for our benefit alone, but they are to expedite the dream He has been holding for us until we could respond to Him in faith and confidence. This dream for us will do far more than care for our personal needs. It places us strategically where we are needed to plant His Kingdom.

The dream is not for us, it is for Him.

His dream satisfies our every need while we are doing His will. His dream for us is unequivocally intertwined with His plan for planet earth. We have now become His portion to the nations, and as such, intricately placed as a part of that plan.

We finally understand that money becomes the least of what we can do in response to the leading of the Lord. We will only be content when He can call upon us anytime to do His bidding. What an incredible personal endorsement of His love when He can say, "Let me call on My friend. He will certainly take care of this for Me."

If you are thrilled to be the portion of the Lord to the nations, you are most certainly dwelling in the Most Holy Place.

6. Are you content to fast food, or is your desire to become God's chosen fast?

Most of us know what the Scriptures call the "true fast," but few of us know the power and significance of this most unusual form of fasting.

But let us be honest. It is so easy to just skip a few meals and expect God to respond to our pious effort to touch Him.

There is a reason that Isaiah spoke the way he did. There is a greater fast. There is a fast of separation, not from food, but from the things that draw us away from our devotion, our love, and our passion.

We must understand that fasting food is an operation of the Holy Place, not the Most Holy Place. The Holy Place is always centered in the activity of the flesh. Man initiates and God responds.

In the Holy Place, we live and act as though we serve a reluctant God. This God seems to always need to be begged, bribed, or badgered into responding to the needs and desires of men who always seem to know better. So man patiently counsels God and then jumps through the necessary hoops to get God to do what he has determined is best.

Holy Place fasting is the extreme measure of an impatient people.

It sends a message to God that He is too slow in His response to us. It is an attempt to prove to Him that we are most serious about what we are requesting and that His immediate response is most urgently requested. We send the message that we do not think He wants to help us, but with the proper amount of correct entreaty, He will respond—reluctantly.

We do not serve a reluctant God.

He does not require self-abasement, nor is He interested in our personal evaluation and advice in a circumstance. The fast of the Most Holy Place is an attitude.

We trust Him and make ourselves available.

Here we lay aside our personal desires to take up the desires of the Lord Jesus. This will ultimately bring the joy of the Lord, which, in the common vernacular, is undisturbed and unshakable happiness. The fast of the Most Holy Place brings purpose and true fulfillment.

Instrument of Righteousness

This fast is a lifestyle and lasts for a lifetime. It is not an event that is restricted to certain times or desperate circumstances, as though by our devout behavior He is moved to intervene in a circumstance in which we need His help. The concept of a reluctant God is quickly replaced by the understanding that He wants to do more than we can possibly understand or imagine. He is truly a God involved in and with the affairs of mankind.

The fast He has chosen is a dedication to His Presence within us. It is a separation from our own will and desires so we can give ourselves to the ministry of the Christ within us to the nations of the world, no matter how He wants to show Himself through us.

The true fast begins when we stop feeding our soul with the fleshy things that prevent us from hearing the voice of the Lord and distract us from yielding to the work of Jesus within us. In the true fast, rather, we yield to the Spirit in order to be the instrument of righteousness we are destined to be. This instrument of righteousness in the hand of the Lord will loosen the bonds of wickedness and allow God to do all He wants to do through those who yield to Him. Remember, we are possessed by One who has the power and passion to undo the bands of oppression, to let the prisoner go free, and to break every yoke.

The true fast begins when we stop feeding our soul with the fleshy things that prevent us from hearing the voice of the Lord.

If we dedicated ourselves to this kind of abandoned lifestyle, putting our prayer toward the work of the Christ within, what would happen to the world? Would to God that His people begin to fast from the desires of the flesh and restrict the sidetracking influences that clutter the spirit and confuse the issues of His purposes. Then we can turn our fast toward the Lord. Would that we were as devoted to responding to the Christ within as we are determined to get our own way through the traditional fast.

Let us fast toward the purposes of God instead of fasting from food.

Jesus inside compels us to divide our bread with the hungry, bringing the homeless poor into the house. This lifestyle of yielding to Him rather than resisting food is a lifestyle that reflects a desire to be found doing His will all the time. It is the compelling evidence that you have become a living sacrifice, holy and pleasing unto the Lord.

So When can I Fast food?

Well, I do not fast to get His attention, to beg for an answer, or to demonstrate piety to Him. But fasting food does play a critical role in our walk with the Lord. God will often call us to a fast when we need to separate ourselves from the distractions of everyday life to more clearly hear from Him. In these instances, fasting helps us to seclude ourselves in the closet of prayer for a season of uninterrupted fellowship with Him. When I fast food, I stay away from the clutter of the world as well, and, as much as possible, the responsibilities of the times. I stay away from television, radio, music, even Christian music, the Internet, and anything else that steals my attention from Him. This clears away the fog of fleshy desire and confusion from my heart and spirit so I can hear His voice and understand His will.

Fasting food helps me shut out the distractions of the world so I can more clearly hear Him. But this separation from the things of the day is also a separation to the Lord. The separation is for me, not the Lord. He is already speaking, I just cannot hear. He has already made a decision in a matter, I am the one who needs to grow quiet enough to hear it.

The Easy Way

In my humanity, I would rather fast for the people in Africa than be sent to Africa. I would rather spend an hour a day in prayer rather than be sent somewhere I do not want to go or be told to do something I do not want to do.

But first and foremost, God sends people, just as He sent His Son on our behalf. The love of our Lord Jesus before He came to earth was not enough. He had to come. His prayers alone could not purchase salvation. Jesus' relationship with His Father did not accomplish deliverance. He had to be born a baby on this planet and do the will of God. The Word had to become flesh. Prayer must ultimately become flesh.

Jesus' prayer in the garden the night before He was crucified was about to be answered by Him, and He knew it. "Nevertheless," He prayed, "not My will, but Your will be done."

Now that He has done the will of His Father, "He is able also to save them to the uttermost that come unto God by him, seeing he ever lives to make intercession for them."

We always want to send words to the Lord, while He wants to send us to the world.

It is always easier to fast food than to make yourself vulnerable to the Presence of God, if you call it being vulnerable. I call it being in the most awesome place a man can be in, a place where God can say, "Nori, do this for Me. Nori, would you give this...go here...pray here...? Nori, would you....?"

The most awesome place to be is in the place where God knows you'll say "yes."

Who Wants to be an Answer to Prayer?

I have learned that when I pray, God often uses me to answer the prayer I have just prayed. I would see people in old, unreliable cars, so I started to pray, "Lord, give that brother a car," and the Lord would say, "Nori, give that brother a car."

I said, "No, Lord, You give that brother a car."

The Lord would say, "I *am* giving him a car—yours."

My wife Cathy and I were in Italy a few years ago where we met and fell in love with a pastor from the south of Italy. This man exudes God's love and forgiveness. He carries power in his hands and love in his heart. But he was driving a car that was not safe for a human to ride in. This car was in a ferocious state. [It was so small, part of me was seated in the front and the other part was in the trunk.] So I was thankful that he was a man of faith.

After I got in the car for the first time, I realized I had to hold the door closed. I would have fastened the seat belt if there had been a seat belt. No wonder he worshiped and prayed so fervently as he drove. To be honest, the Presence of God was incredible in the car. I would have been able to enjoy it more, though, if he had kept his eyes open as he drove and at least one hand on the wheel. I quickly understood why there were so many dents and dings on the car. Shouting through the exhaust that poured in from a missing window, I told my wife, "This pastor needs a new car." We both laughed. But the Lord had the last laugh when the pastor made a quite unexpected left turn that almost rolled me out of the car. After regaining my composure, I complained to the Lord, "Lord, this brother needs a new car."

And the Lord said, "You're right, he does need a car." I already knew what that meant: "Get the brother a car."

After this happened three or four times, I began to realize I had to make a decision as to whether I would continue to pray or close my heart to being used by the Lord to answer the prayers I myself was voicing.

The fast Isaiah saw is a single-minded determination to do the will of God. It is a separation, to be sure. But it is not a separation from food; it is a separation from everything that distracts us from hearing His voice. It is a fast from the lusts of the flesh that prevent us from being ready anytime He calls out our name.

Isaiah's fast sends us, the bearers of the Christ and His salvation, to a hurting and dying world. It is the fast that changes the world.

So fasting food for personal gain is the function of the Holy Place, where we try to force God into doing something we want to be done.

Sometimes, fasting food is often a fleshy act of penance when we have done something so bad we think the Blood alone can't cover it. It is easier to fast food than it is to present ourselves as a living sacrifice to be used of Him.

The point is that fasting in no way is an excuse that relieves us of our ultimate responsibility and the liberating joy of simply saying "yes" to Him.

The most exciting attitude we can have is an attitude of personal dedication to the Lord and separation from the noise of the world and the flesh. In this place, God knows you'll say yes.

"Is this not the fast which I chose?" the Lord asks through the prophet. "To loosen the bonds of wickedness..." Deep in your heart, you know that this is your fervent desire and prayer:

"...to undo the bands of the yoke, to let the oppressed go free, to break every yoke." (This certainly sounds just like you.) "To divide your bread with the hungry, to bring the homeless poor into your home. When you see the naked to cover him?"

If your heart burns at the possibility to carry this freedom and deliverance to those around you, then you are already a priest of the Presence. If your fast is a continual dedication to the Lord, keeping yourself available to Him at all times for His use, you already dwell in the Most Holy Place.

7. What are you waiting for: the Lord's appearing in the sky, or the Lord's appearing in you?

We all want to see Jesus.

Most of us are taught that His appearing will occur one day when He returns in the clouds. We will be caught up with Him, and we will forever be with Him.

We hold on for that blessed day of His appearing. We pray for that day. But some are content to wait for either His appearing in the air or when they stand before the Lord after they are called home.

There is a much more exciting event than that: His appearing in us. It is largely ignored by many, dare I say, most. He will appear in us long before we see Him appear in the sky. Our Lord wants to show Himself to the world through us long before He displays Himself in the clouds. In fact, He is forever showing Himself through us to those all around us.

Jesus taught us to pray, "Thy Kingdom come, Thy will be done on earth as it is in heaven." The Kingdom comes when the King comes. There cannot be a Kingdom without a King. When the King appears, the Kingdom comes. He plants the wonders of His life, His Kingdom, in us each day, each moment we are willing to say "yes" to His will and "no" to our own fleshy desires.

When we discover that He is appearing in us, our religious gymnastics to gain His approval give way to rest and peace.

As always, the issue is one of theology. Some are interested in seeing the Lord in the sky, while others want to be the lamp of the Lord through whom He will shine eternal light upon a dying world.

One requires only eyes; the second requires heart. All eyes will see Him when He appears in the sky, but only the broken and humble will see Him within. He is impassioned by the love of His Father and driven by compassion for the masses. His heart carries healing to the nations.

He is not looking for preachers or more religious leaders. He is looking for the average person, the one who does not get a second glance by those who see them. He is looking for the clerk, the teacher, the factory worker, the contractor, the lawyer, the student, the stay-at-home mom. These are the ones through whom He will change the world, one person, one life, one neighborhood, one church, one hamlet, one village, one town, one heart at a time.

Are you waiting for the Lord to appear in you, or are you waiting for Him to appear in the sky?

He will appear in us long before we see Him appear in the sky.

If you are waiting for His appearing in the sky, I cannot help you. For we know that He will appear sometime, at a point of His choosing, for all the world to see. At this appearing, He will gather His own to Himself and we will ever be with the Lord.

But some of you want to be a lamp for the Lord. You will experience His appearing each day as you faithfully give Him control of the reins of your life. For He longs to show Himself to the hungry, the lonely, the needy, the dying. You are the lamp through whom He will appear continuously to a world in desperate need. Through you and me, the lamp of the Lord, He will gather the nations to Himself, forgiving their sins and breaking the power of iniquity in their lives.

If you want the Lord to appear in you and through you, where you are right now, you are most undoubtedly already seated in the Most Holy Place.

8. Do you flow in a particular gift of the Spirit, or are you open for the fullness of Christ to manifest through your life?

Who has the gift of prophecy? Who has the gift of tongues? Who has gifts of healing, and who has discernment? Who has the gift of hospitality, and who has the gift of faith?

Now, more importantly, who is content with what he has? Who is content to be identified with a portion of Christ when the fullness of Christ is available?

Is it heresy to believe there is more in Christ than what we have been allowed to believe? Is anyone among us willing to admit there is still more to experience from the throne of God?

If you are at least somewhat like me, you will admit to some level of discontent with what is and what could be if only we moved beyond what we have been taught.

I carried feelings of near condemnation for several years merely because I could not be satisfied with what I thought was all that this gospel message had to offer. There had to be more to it than what I was experiencing. There had to be a different path than the one demonstrated to me over the years.

I often cried before the Lord in great frustration. I loved the Lord. I trusted Him. I owe Him everything for all eternity; I owe Him my very life. I never wanted to sound ungrateful. But why did I feel so thirsty all the time? Why was there this gnawing inside that could not be satisfied even with all the things I was doing? After all, I was dutifully involved with all the things I was told I should be doing. There had to be more.

> *I am possessed. Pure and simple. I do not need titles to the left of my name or letters of the alphabet to the right of my name. I am crucified with Christ.*

I must admit that I prayed some strange things to the Lord in those days: "Lord, if this is what You died for, I am sorry to say that I believe You wasted Your time."

Again, "Lord Jesus, this cannot possibly be the Church You are building!"

Yes, there is yet more I said to Him in my lonely frustration: "Jesus, You mean this is all there is? This is it?"

I know that some may feel these prayers inappropriate. Maybe they were. But they started me on a journey of discovery that continues to change my life and challenge my heart. It has opened the heavens and the heart of God to me. It has helped me to understand His wonderful intentions for humanity more clearly. It caused me to discover the true God of love and compassion, replacing a cheap human imitation of a God of judgment and legalism.

Yes, He does have more. He is more than anything we have ever thought possible. For in this journey, I found a God of fullness instead of a God of limitations. He never really intended to give us only a piece of Himself. He gave us all that He is. I really can do all things through Christ who strengthens me. For it is He who is at work inside of me to do His good pleasure.

Unlimited God

Now, I understand myself better as well. Now, if I am limited, I am limited by my own need to be identified with a particular function. If I am limited, I am limited by my own desire for a title. If I am restrained, I am restrained by my own unwillingness to move in God beyond my experience. The limitation is in me; it is not in Him.

The moment we are willing to identify with Him more than our own position, gifts, or title, we find ourselves free from the trappings of man and free to serve Him in complete liberty.

We Are Free

I am never limited or restrained by my occupation. Quite the contrary, my occupation is exactly where He wants me to take Him. Christ lives His life through me, and He can do through me whatever He wants to do. I do not need recognition, award, or financial remuneration. I do not serve Him for profit or to get someone to a church service. I am responding to Him who possesses me, and I will not restrict Him by what I or someone else has branded me. I am possessed. Pure and simple. I do not need titles to the left of my name or letters of the alphabet to the right of my name. I am crucified with Christ. It is no longer I who live but Christ who lives in me, and the life I now live I live in Him.

If you covet the fullness of Christ and are not content with the limitations religion imposes upon you, I am certain that He is at work in your heart as you sit at the right hand of your Father on the Mercy Seat of the Most Holy Place.

9. Is your destiny a destination, or is your destiny a way of life?

Destiny is the current buzz word in Christianity. Every one is talking about destiny. But as usual, we have attributed to this beautiful word a very human, very selfish definition. Most of us are concerned about destiny insofar as it concerns our future, our success, our personal security. But destiny in Christ is far different from the selection of a career or a particular educational track.

Destiny Can Never be a Destination

Destiny is not about where we end up. It is about yielding to Him, who is the author and the finisher, the beginning and the end. He is our way, our destiny. He is the creator of more destiny than all of humanity can experience in all of the lifetimes we will collectively ever live.

If your destiny is a destination, you will succeed in one area and limit your experience to that narrow thing you have determined is your destiny. You will most likely miss the awe and wonder of the multifaceted dream that He has certainly dreamed for your life.

It is certain God has dreamed many dreams for you. There are many adventures for you to go on with Him. So destiny begs a redefinition in keeping with who we are in Him and in keeping with His intention for us from the beginning.

The destiny of those who call upon Him is to be conformed to His image and likeness. He wants to shine through us for all the world to see His glory. He wants the hungry to feed from our love and the lonely to be encouraged with our words. He will bless the poor and heal the sick as He works through simple folks like you and me. He will set the prisoner free and forgive the iniquity of fallen man, all through His people.

He will love and not judge, gather and scatter, bring hope and shatter fear.

He will demonstrate mercy and find the absolute best in the heart of every man.

He will bring the good news of His own redemption of mankind and declare to people everywhere that their warfare is ended.

He will do this through you and me every day we live and breathe. He will do it through us as we shop and as we work. He will show Himself at the most unusual times, as He sends us here and there, opening doors that no man can open for himself and giving us favor that we cannot gain for ourselves.

He will give us courage when we should fear, direction when we should be lost, and words when we should be speechless.

He causes us to stand when we want to run, love when we want to hate, and hope even when the world screams to us to be in despair.

Our destiny is to live in the "yes" of God. It is there, in His "yes," that we find ourselves going wherever He leads and doing whatever He wants us to do. We go from glory to glory as we respond in eager and faithful obedience to Him. He changes us while we change the world. For we do not go in our own strength or wisdom. We do not go as a reward for piety, good works, or religious activity. We go because He has dreamed a dream for us. We go in response to the destiny He has purposefully and meticulously designed for us.

This whole concept is far from new, however. To be sure, it sounds very familiar to the words of Jesus, who taught to seek His Kingdom first, and everything else will be provided.

For in this realm you will discover that your success is not in what you do but in who you are letting live through you. It is no longer you who lives; rather He is truly living His dynamic life through you. He is relentlessly pouring His love and compassion out to the world through the likes of average folk like you and me, who have no desire for anything but to be hidden in Him, who is hidden in us.

When destiny is tied to all the dreams He has dreamed for you, success cannot help but follow wherever you go.

Heaven is my destination, it is not my destiny. Many will reach their destination, but few will fulfill their destiny.

If your destiny is a way of life, there is a high probability that you are already a priest of the Presence. You are already seated with Him within the veil of your flesh, in the "yes" of God, the Most Holy Place.

10. Do you look for a prophetic word, or are you becoming a prophetic word?

Jesus is the prophetic Word to the nations for every generation that has, that is, and will ever live.

When the Word became flesh, He became the demonstration, the living evidence that all that had been spoken by those who came before Him was accurate. His appearing shut the mouths of the naysayers and proved the words of the prophets once and for all. His coming was a death sentence to sin and the powers of hell. It was a victory cry to all who awaited Him, both living and dead.

Now the prophetic Word, spoken from the heart of God Himself, had become flesh and walked among humanity. Now there would be nothing satan or any of his minions could do to stop Him. Eternity had become flesh and blood, and as His enemies would soon discover, He could not be destroyed. He had delivered the power of eternity into this realm, where He would live and rule forever. Here He would declare His Kingdom and here He would build it in the hearts of mortal men and women who would be the very throne of His Majesty, the seat of mercy to the world.

Their very existence would carry the prophetic essence of eternity and point forever to Him who occupies the throne within them.

Mere mortals had become prophetic words to the nations.

Jesus embodied the heart and passion of the Father to redeem a people for His own possession, for His own purposes in the earth. Jesus was the constant reminder to a busy and preoccupied world that He was and is in the earth, continuously redeeming it one soul at a time. He is waiting, calling, loving, and gathering. He is the light that will not go out. It may be outlawed from schools and governments. It can be ignored by the media, but He still shines in the hearts of those in whom He lives and moves and exists.

He is the moment-by-moment demonstration that He does not take orders from the systems of this world and does not take kindly to those who build their own kingdoms under the guise of the King of Kings.

He was and is the prophetic Word to the nations.

Now in light of this immutable truth of His single-minded intention, I have discovered that I have a choice in the matter. Will I be a prophetic word to the world, or will I spend my life looking for one?

Jesus is the real-time evidence that He does not take orders from the systems of this world and does not take kindly to those who build their own kingdoms under the guise of the King of Kings.

What do I really believe? Will I be bread to the hungry, or will I be a needy one, always looking for bread? Holy Place believers gather fruit for the day. Most Holy Place believers bear fruit for the nations.

Those who are possessed by Him are by the new nature within them a living prophetic word to the world. Everything we are, everything we do, everything we say will point to Him who has redeemed us and loves us.

Our lives are a living testimony that there are those who are in open communication with Him and that He wants the same from all humanity.

But this is far from where most believers live. The notion that we can live strong and stable lives is simply too hard to accept for many. The sense that the Lord will speak to our hearts clearly enough to provide direction and hope, even in the most difficult situations, appears quite unbelievable. For the average believer, the idea that we can be witnesses of His life and love during the most tumultuous of times has always been a fairy tale.

We have lived our lives far short of the glory He came to implant in our hearts. We have been taught that that is the way it is supposed to be. So we are content to live in weakness and doubt. We think it somehow proves our holiness to live on the brink of poverty and confusion.

We have missed the point.

Our goal should not be to simply hang on until the end. Our goal is not to toil through life from church service to church service, somehow gathering enough scraps of spiritual nourishment to struggle through until the next service. I am possessed by Someone all-powerful. He is daily waiting for me to yield to Him that His glory might shine through me.

I am not looking for a prophetic word. Because Christ lives within and lives His life through me, I am a prophetic word to the nations of the world.

If your heart is to be a prophetic word, you have moved from the riddles and uncertainty of the Holy Place. You have discovered that you are seated with Him within the veil of your own humanity, your own heart, where you sit with Him on the seat of mercy, in the Most Holy Place.

Looking at Your Results

See, now that wasn't so hard, was it? I was right, wasn't I? You loved this test. If you are like most who have taken this test, you are in shock and awe at what you have discovered about yourself. You may even be wondering if these results are an accurate appraisal of who you really are and what you really believe. But you will get over that ridiculous notion. For that thought is just residue from your former conditioning to deny everything you feel, as well as to accept everything you have been told.

The Old Covenant heart may be deceitful above all things, but the New Covenant heart is a completely different heart. It is absolutely new. The heart of the New Covenant is engraved by the finger of God. Your heart is being softened, taught, and empowered by the Lord Himself. Now you are no longer compelled to completely ignore the thoughts and desires of your heart, always assuming those thoughts and desires are somehow evil or self-centered. Now you are judging your thoughts and desires. You are discerning their source and thus their authenticity. You now understand that He is building His Kingdom inside of you. He is tearing down the old and replacing it with Himself. Everything you feel is not automatically evil or automatically righteous. His Spirit is at work within you. Thank God that His work within is crowding out the evil that once ruled and deceived you. You really are being changed from one degree of glory to another.

Now you can be certain: He is changing you while you are changing the world.

Now you know. He loves you. You love Him. You are where you have always wanted to be—in progress, of course, but seated with Him, resting with Him, praying with Him, changing the world with Him.

You have passed the test. But I never doubted that you would. I know your heart. It is just like mine.

Chapter 16 Scripture References

I John 2:8 PEB
Philemon 1:21 NKJV
Colossians 1:27 PEB
Romans 10:9 PEB
Hebrews 13:15
Son of Solomon 2:16 NAS
Mark 14:36 PEB
John 1:14 PEB

Hebrews 9:24 PEB
Acts 17:28 PEB
Mark 16:19 PEB
Matthew 27:51
Romans 12:1 NAS
Ephesians 1:4 PEB
Matthew 5:15 PEB
Philemon 2:15 NKJV

The truth of who you are is more powerful than you have been permitted to believe.

*I do
not fear the
consequences
of a relentless
pursuit of
this divine
reality.*

CHAPTER 17

The Secret of Revolution

I know, I know, revolution is a pretty strong word. So I hope you are not one of those people who read the last chapter before you read the rest of the book. It will be hard to understand and appreciate this otherwise. So please, if you have not read the book, please stop now, and read it from the beginning. Thank you!!

The transition from the system of religion to the Church that Jesus is building is closer than most think. For it is only a decision away. It begins when the decision is made to be a true shepherd of the sheep, the household of God. A shepherd leads the sheep to cool waters and green pastures, which are always representative of His Manifest Presence. He is the One who nourishes and constructs within us a home for Himself to live for as long as we draw breath. The Church Jesus is building releases His people to be all God has dreamed for them to be. It teaches forgiveness and freedom from guilt, fear, regret and the slavish works of the flesh. This Church is built by Jesus alone and His Kingdom is the natural result of people who are in love with Him and are free to discover the wonders of His love and power.

This Church is like a highway, a roadway. It will be called the Highway of Holiness. The unclean will not travel on it. It will only be for him who walks that way. The foolish will not be able to wander on it.

There will be no lion there either, nor will any vicious beasts walk on it. No devourers will walk among His people on this highway. For this road is for the Redeemed of the Lord who will return with joyful shouting to Zion, the place of His Manifest

Presence. They will find gladness and joy there; sorrow and sighing will flee away. They will live in everlasting joy. This was the intention of the Lord when He sent His Son on our behalf.

This is what will happen when the decision is made to yield to Jesus so He can build His Church through us and among us. The prisoners are then finally set free. I am not talking about those who are the prisoners of sin or iniquity. I am not talking about those who are bound by demonic forces.

You may find this hard to believe, but there is a force that is far more sinister than either of these, as awful as they are.

I am talking about people who have been bound for years by the belief systems of those who have never seen the Lord, but nonetheless have contrived great theological treatises about Him and His apparent activity or inactivity in the earth. These are the so-called bastions of intellectual religious knowledge that dictate the dos and don'ts of religious activity to the rest of us. They determine the parameters within which the common folk can safely worship and fellowship with God.

Their academic plumbline decides for the rest of us who is, and is not, a heretic. Based on their own intellectual assent of who they believe God is, and apart from actual experience, they control the growth of true spirituality and experience through fear and intimidation.

They fully expect the common people to blindly follow their enlightened path, regardless of what real-life experience tells those who are truly hungry seekers. It is of no concern that His Presence draws them beyond the realm of conventional thought. Despite the reality of such experiences, the commoner is fully expected to limit his experience with God to the accepted intellectually contrived boundaries of the "Dead Theologians Society."

And most of us do accept those boundaries. Most of us will reluctantly deny or explain away even the most dynamic experiences we have had to maintain a good relationship with these so-called shepherds. For who wants to be labeled a heretic? As long as they control the bully pulpit, they control the conversation and the agenda. The "Dead Theologians Society" wields influence and commands respect, not because of the truth it bears, but because of the "deity" it has become.

"Dead Theologians Society?" you may ask. We have to remember that contemporary Christianity is the product of theologians who wrote hundreds of years ago. Their studies have been venerated and passed on from generation to generation. The more they are passed on, the more canon-like they become. Soon it is difficult to distinguish between these theories and the Scriptures themselves. These canon-like doctrines prohibit the spiritual growth that should be the normal experience of the daily Christian life. By determining what God can, can't, will, and won't do, they prevent the purposes of God from moving forward in the hearts of His people and in the earth in general.

Instead of the adventure of seeing His mercies new every morning, we are locked into the words of someone we do not know. Yet we commit our beliefs to these guys as though they were the Lord Himself. It is amazing. We would not entrust our physical lives into the hands of strangers, yet we will commit our spiritual lives and future into the hands of absolute strangers we only know from dusty old history books.

We dutifully attend meetings once, twice, or three times a week, subjecting ourselves to what we have been led to believe will bring us close to the Lord. But in reality much of this stuff ensures we will never experience His glory or a genuine personal relationship with the One we so desperately love. If that were not bad enough, we also bring our children so that from a very impressionable age, they too are indoctrinated into the ways of "The Society." By the time they are older, what they are being taught, they would not dare challenge The Society's authority or teaching.

Evangelicals often chide their Catholic brethren because Catholics make the pope equal with God. Yet evangelicals hold the teaching of the "Dead Theologians Society" in the same high regard. Those who do not agree with these deep thinkers are not excommunicated, as some Catholics are, but rather they are branded as rebels or worse.

The Pressure is On

The Church Jesus is building always will place the purpose of God for the people as the first priority of ministry.

Is the Book Closed?

As this distinguished society disseminates their work, the line between the doctrines of men and the truth of Scripture becomes so blurred that only the theologians themselves, quite conveniently, can discern the difference. This leaves the common believer at the mercy of the theorist who has never seen the Lord.

Is there nothing new to be seen in the Scriptures?

Is the Word of God so shallow that it is so easily comprehended and categorized?

Is the Book closed?

Have we exhausted its wonder?

Have we discovered all of its mystery? Is it really alive as we confess it is?

Who then can say all that can be seen has been discovered? Who then can declare themselves the final authority? Are we to believe religious bureaucrats who have proclaimed themselves the heirs of truth? Have they earned the right to establish themselves as the dynasty of church leadership? I think not, for I do not believe the "royal priesthood" so lovingly spoken of in the Scriptures refers to an elitist dynasty schooled only in the ways perpetual stagnation of the living holy Writ.

God Confounds the Intellectual

While the Word is final, our heart understanding and our life experience of it is elementary at best. We spend endless hours discussing genealogies and issues that are moot in the grand scheme of Scripture's true message—the reality of the Lord and the one-on-one interactive fellowship He covets with His people. The distracting issues in which these great thinkers pride themselves do nothing to quench the thirsting of the soul and only prove the emptiness of such truly trivial pursuits.

But even more absurd is the notion that God will stay within the boundaries set by mere mortal men. What arrogance dwells in the heart of man that makes him think he can determine the activity of God? What is it in him that makes mortal man suppose God will dutifully respond to his finite theology and self-centered religion?

God ignores academic assertions devoid of experience and passion in favor of the one who has humbly responded to His love. For there is nothing our Lord will not do in, through, and for the one who has yielded himself to Christ who dwells within.

Our Lord's thoughts are higher than the thoughts of man, even the thoughts of many men. The greatest thinkers among us are but fools in the sight of God. There is no understanding of His ways apart from genuine, day-by-day experience with the living God.

God's People Do Something

God will have those who will not settle for these meager attempts to pass on such foolishness. He will have those who understand the heart of God, yearning to express Himself to a dying world. He will have those who will do more than merely agree with words such as those written here. For it is true, the heart must be stirred. But a stirred heart is not enough. It must be stirred to action. Believing that something must be done is not enough. Knowing the corruption of the religious system is not enough.

Merely believing that change must happen does not absolve us from the need to actually respond to the Spirit of the Lord inside. Many believers are so trapped in the system they cannot imagine breaking free from the things that prevent the dream God has for them blossoming in their lives.

But we are not exempt from action simply because we agree that revolution is necessary. Volumes of books are written and loved by those who will never do what needs to be done. They are satisfied that they have read, and accept that change is crucial, but they have no strength to be the ones who challenge the system as it is.

But there will be those who do not fear the consequences of a relentless pursuit of this divine reality. There are those possessed among us who will release the Spirit of the One who possesses them. They will allow the Christ within to enter their temple, as it were, and turn over the tables of those who are at ease in Zion.

They will demonstrate the love and passionate desire of the Lord for His people. They will live in God's chosen fast. They will allow their words to become keys that unlock the hearts and minds of millions who live in the ugly grasp of an anti-Christ system of religion that only knows how to condemn, rebuke, deceive and separate. They will proclaim the mysteries of the ages, releasing God's love and mercy upon the masses who are desperate to come home to Father's house.

True Revolutionaries

These are the true revolutionaries of our time. They live among us. They will not be content simply to hear the words of true deliverance and freedom. They will actually set the prisoners free. These gentle giants have had enough of the shame and fear and religious death sentences that are passed on by men who belong to the "Dead Theologians Society."

The Lord's voice once shook the earth; yet once more He will shake not only the earth but also the heaven. Everything that is man-contrived will be removed so that all that remains is of the Kingdom He Himself is building. For He does not need the sweat of our brow or the advice of an intellectually advanced culture. He is looking for our cooperation, a people through whom He can completely live His life, expressing His mercy, compassion, love, and healing salve to the nations of the world.

He will have a people through whom He can set the captives free, not through the tickling of the senses, but through the demonstration of His love by means of humble and contrite hearts. It is then that there will be the removal of those things that can be shaken—the man-made things—in order that those things that cannot be shaken may remain.

Thy Kingdom Come

Only the Kingdom He is building will never be shaken. Some would have you believe otherwise, but that is only because they arrogantly believe they hold your purse strings or control your destiny. The heart of the king is in the hand of the Lord; the nay or yea on any issue is from His throne.

He holds the keys to your future.

We have received a Kingdom that cannot be shaken. This is the Kingdom to seek!

I, for one, am not satisfied to agree with God only in the quiet of my own prayer closet. I must be a voice among many on the earth that cries out to everyone who will listen, "If you have died with Christ to the elementary principles of the world, why, as if you were living in the world, do you submit yourself to the decrees of legalism that look holy enough, but will never ignite the glory of God within? He whom the Son sets free is free indeed."

But here is the secret to revolution. It begins in the hearts of those whose love and passion for Him can never be quenched by threat, manipulation, exclusion, or religious piety.

This revolution begins among men when, "yes" is heard in the heavens and in the earth. It grows in strength as it grows in the hearts of believers who allow revolution to take place in their own hearts, lead by the One whose revolution has changed the world for all time.

These are the people who will change the world. These are the ones who will change the Church. They will see the precious dream God has for them come to fullness in their lives. They will be part of the greatest dream of God's heart and rejoice with Him as the kingdoms of this world become the Kingdoms of our God and of His Christ. His revolution in and among men will establish His reign on this planet forever and ever.

These people will shout it from the housetops. They will contend for His love, His mercy, His compassion and His salvation. They will demonstrate this love and compassion to the whole world. They will shine among religions because they do not carry the sound of condemnation. Rather, they sing the song of the Savior, the song of deliverance, the song of never-ending mercy.

"Thy kingdom come O King Jesus, bring your Kingdom to this earth. May you build it, beginning with me. Then grant that I may love you always and then do with me whatever you will."

Chapter 17 Scripture References

Isaiah 35: 8,9 and 10 KJV	Jeremiah 5:21 NKJV
Lamentations 3:21-24 NKJV	John 1:14 PEB
Romans 8:1 NKJV	Ephesians 5:25 PEB
Ephesians 1:9 NKJV	John 7:37-38 PEB
Isaiah 55 8-9 NKJV	James 2:17 PEB
Romans 8:4 PEB	John 8:36 PEB
Matthew 16:19 PEB	Joel 2:28 NKJV

There are those among us who do not fear the consequences of a relentless pursuit of this divine reality.

Contact Information

DON NORI

c/o Destiny Image Publishers
167 Walnut Bottom Rd.
Shippensburg, PA 17257

Ph: 717-532-3040   Ext: 124

E-mail: dfn@destinyimage.com

To understand where you are going, first you must know where you have been...

SECRETS OF THE
MOST HOLY PLACE VOL. 1
BY DON NORI

Here is a prophetic parable you will read again and again. The winds of God are blowing, drawing you to His Life within the Veil of the Most Holy Place. There you begin to see as you experience a depth of relationship your heart has yearned for. This book is a living, dynamic experience with God.

ISBN 1-56043-076-1

A story of True Love...
and the fulfillment it brings!

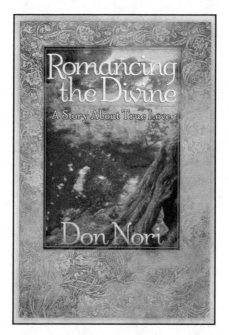

ROMANCING THE DIVINE
BY DON NORI

Romancing the Divine is a tale of every person's journey to find the reality of God. It is a tale of hope, a search for eternal love, and for all the possibilities we have always imagined would be the conclusion of such a search. In this story you will most assuredly recognize your own search for God, and discover the divine fulfillment that His love brings.

ISBN 0-7684-2053-9

The secret to knowing God's plans and desires for your personal destiny!

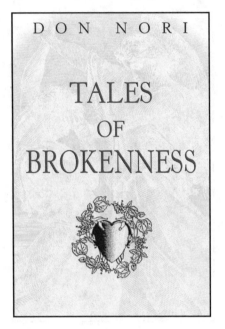

TALES OF BROKENNESS
BY DON NORI

Brokenness—the disdain of tyrants and the wonder of kings. Her mystery has eluded the intellectual and empowered the noble of heart. From her bosom flow the power and compassion to change the world.

In *Tales of Brokenness* you'll meet this companion who never forgets her need of mercy, never forgets the grace that flows on her behalf. She is the secret to knowing God's plans and desires and to finding your way to your personal destiny.

ISBN 0-7684-2074-1

Also by Don Nori:

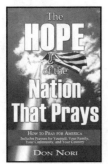

THE HOPE OF THE NATION THAT PRAYS
BY DON NORI

The Hope of the Nation That Prays offers an encouraging look at God's love and His will for America. Take a step back in time with prayers from historical figures who have experienced extraordinary answers to prayers in times of crisis. Features prayers from such great leaders as Martin Luther King, Jr., Abraham Lincoln, and many others.

ISBN 0-7684-3045-3

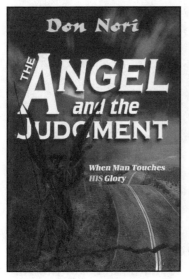

THE ANGEL AND
THE JUDGMENT
BY DON NORI

Few understand the power of our judgments, or the aftermath of the words we speak in thoughtless, emotional pain. In this powerful story about a preacher and an angel, you'll see how the earth is changed by the words we utter in secret.

ISBN 1-56043-154-7

Also by Don Nori:
Ground-breaking teachings on DVD!

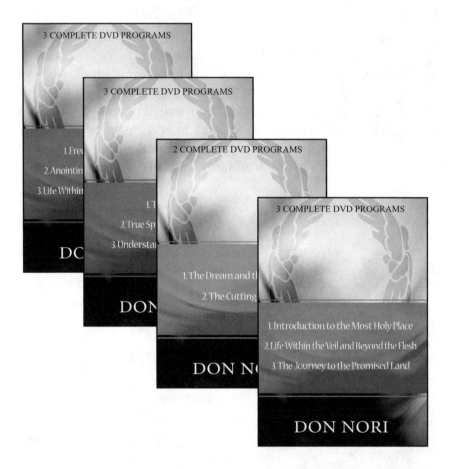

Don Nori's most popular teachings, now available on DVD! Each studio-produced DVD contains at least 2 teachings by Don Nori that originally aired on television and satellite stations around the world.

Also by Don Nori:
Ground-breaking teachings on CD!

For the first time ever you can own Don Nori's most popular teachings on the Most Holy Place on CD! Experience the power of walking through the temple as you uncover the secrets of the Most Holy Place.

Additional copies of this book and other book titles from DESTINY IMAGE are available at your local bookstore.

For a bookstore near you, call 1-800-722-6774.

Send a request for a catalog to:

Destiny Image® Publishers, Inc.

P.O. Box 310
Shippensburg, PA 17257-0310

*"Speaking to the Purposes of God for This
Generation and for the Generations to Come"*

For a complete list of our titles,
visit us at www.destinyimage.com